Fish and Wildlife Research 7

Chironomidae of the Southeastern United States: A Checklist of Species and Notes on Biology, Distribution, and Habitat

By Patrick L. Hudson
    David R. Lenat
    Broughton A. Caldwell
    David Smith

UNITED STATES DEPARTMENT OF THE INTERIOR
FISH AND WILDLIFE SERVICE
Washington, D.C. • 1990

Contents

Chironomidae of the Southeastern United States:
A Checklist of Species and Notes on Biology, Distribution, and Habitat[1]

by

Patrick L. Hudson[2]

U.S. Fish and Wildlife Service
National Fisheries Research Center—Great Lakes
1451 Green Road
Ann Arbor, Michigan 48105

David R. Lenat

North Carolina Department of Natural Resources
Archdale Building, P.O. Box 27687
Raleigh, North Carolina 27611

Broughton A. Caldwell

2382 Rockwood Way
Stone Mountain, Georgia 30087

and

David Smith

U.S. Environmental Protection Agency
Ecological Support Branch
College Station Road
Athens, Georgia 30613

ABSTRACT.—We provide a current listing of the species of midges (Diptera:Chironomidae) in the southeastern United States (Alabama, Florida, Georgia, North Carolina, South Carolina, and Tennessee). This checklist should aid in research on this group of insects, which have often proved useful in the assessment of water quality. We document each species' distribution and general habitat and provide the best taxonomic reference to facilitate the identification or description of species in that genus. Changes in nomenclature, unique ecological traits, bibliographic sources, or other items of information are summarized in a paragraph on each genus. Of the 10 subfamilies currently recognized in the Chironomidae, 7 occur in the Southeast. The chironomid fauna of the six southeastern States now consists of 164 described genera and 479 described species. In addition we have listed 14 genera and 245 species that are tentatively noted as undescribed

---

[1]Contribution 750 of the National Fisheries Research Center—Great Lakes, U.S. Fish and Wildlife Service, 1451 Green Road, Ann Arbor, Mich. 48105.
[2]Former address: U.S. Fish and Wildlife Service, Southeast Reservoir Investigations, Clemson, S.C. 29631.

or that have been illustrated but not officially described. Regional distribution of the principal subfamilies indicated that the species of Chironominae and Tanypodinae were concentrated in the coastal region, whereas the Orthocladiinae were evenly distributed from the coast to the mountains. Considering the major habitats (lakes, rivers, and streams), Tanypodinae were about evenly distributed; Orthocladiinae were more predominant in streams and Chironominae in lakes.

"What sort of insects do you rejoice in, where you come from?"
the Gnat inquired.
"I don't rejoice in insects at all," Alice explained; . . . "But
I can tell you the names of some of them."
"Of course they answer to their names?" the Gnat remarked
carelessly.
"I never knew them to do it."
"What's the use of their having names," the Gnat said, "if
they won't answer to them?"
"No use to them," said Alice; "but it's useful to the people
that name them, I suppose. . . ."

—Lewis Carroll
Through the Looking-Glass, 1871

We here give you the names of chironomids (which are sometimes referred to as gnats) and hope they will be "useful to the people that name them."

The North American Chironomidae, a large dipteran family with predominantly aquatic immature stages, have often been used for the assessment of water quality since the early 1950's. Much of the taxonomic work required in support of this research has been carried out in the eastern United States—particularly in the Southeast. The late Selwyn Roback of the Academy of Natural Sciences of Philadelphia led this taxonomic thrust in the Southeast with 22 papers, mainly on immature chironomids in the subfamily Tanypodinae, but including a definitive monograph on the adults (Roback 1971). Ole Saether of the University of Bergen, Norway, has published 24 works, mainly on the subfamily Orthocladiinae; and William and Elizabeth Beck of the Florida State Board of Health have contributed 10 papers on the Chironomidae. Much taxonomic work has been supported by field biologists who in their routine water-quality assessments collected extensive material for systematists. Although such taxonomic brokerage is not unique to the Southeast, it has provided especially large numbers of specimens from the Southeast to systematists worldwide. As a result, the chironomids of this region are perhaps better known than those from any other region of North America.

The main purpose of this compilation is to provide a listing of the chironomid species of the southeastern United States. In addition, we have been collecting chironomids since the 1960's and many of the distributional data and habitat notes are unpublished or scattered in informal reports of our respective agencies. We describe distribution and general habitat for each species and provide the best taxonomic references available to facilitate the identification or description of species in each genus. Changes in nomenclature, unique ecological traits, and other items of information are briefly summarized for each genus.

Nomenclature and Taxonomy

Ten subfamilies and 24 tribes are currently recognized in the Chironomidae (Ashe 1983). Seven of the subfamilies occur in the Southeast (tribes are not specifically used in our descriptions). Ashe (1983) listed 355 valid genus-group names but later (Ashe et al. 1987) recognized only 307 by excluding genera of doubtful status. Most genera can now be identified by using the keys in Wiederholm (1989) for males and those of Saether (1977a) for females. Generic determinations for the immature stages were provided in the Holarctic keys by Wiederholm (1983, 1986) or in keys by Coffman and

Ferrington (1984). The works by Pinder (1978) and Cranston (1982a) on the British fauna also provided useful keys and descriptions.

Most taxonomic problems that plagued early chironomid researchers have been corrected by others. The genera *Tendipes* and *Pelopia* have been formally suppressed, although some authors still persist in recognizing them. A full description of this problem and several others was given by Ashe (1983). Generic limits in the family have evolved from a system of a few large genera containing many species to a system of many genera containing fewer species. This propensity for smaller genera was a result of finding morphological differences in the immature stages that were much more pronounced than those in the adults, which were often examined exclusively by earlier taxonomists. A general rule is that if each of the three life stages—larva, pupa, and adult—falls into a relatively discernible group, the group is treated as a genus. Subgeneric groups are usually established when one or more of the life stages in a group of species are difficult to separate, whereas one or both of the other stages show consistent morphological differences (Hamilton et al. 1969). These nomenclatorial decisions should continue to evolve as more material is collected and all life stages become known.

Guide to the Checklist

The arrangement of the subfamilies in Tables 1–4 follows Saether (1977a). Generic names within subfamilies, and species within genera, are listed alphabetically. State distributional records are from the literature, from our collections, and from personal communications with a number of aquatic biologists of the Southeast and elsewhere. Names of those who contributed information in personal communications are shown in the text and their affiliations in the Acknowledgments. Most of the species records are based on collections of adults, because species keys for immatures are still lacking for most genera. In addition to the described species, we list distinctive immature stages such as Roback's (1987a) *Labrundinia* sp. 4 (Table 1). This listing largely concerns distinct taxa based on major revisions where the author has provided a written description and figure. When additional materials become available these forms will probably be described as new species.

Enough collections of adults have been made in the Southeast to at least establish the presence of the genus or species in the region. When only immature stages are available to establish a generic presence—

Table 1. *Summary of distribution and habitat for Tanypodinae in the southeastern United States. Habitat: L = lakes (natural, impoundments, swamps), M = marine, R = river (>12 m wide), S = streams (⩽12 m wide), Sp = seeps or springs, T = terrestrial. Regions (see Figure for locations): C = Coastal Plain including Sandhills, I = Interior Upland, M = Mountains (Ridge and Valley and Appalachian), P = Piedmont Plateau.*

Genus, subgenus, species, and author	State[a]						Habitat	Region	Reference[b]
	AL	FL	GA	NC	SC	TN			
Ablabesmyia									15
(*Ablabesmyia*)									
aspera Roback		x	x		x	x	LS	CM	
hauberi Beck and Beck	x	x	x	x	x		LRS	CP	
janta (Roback)		x	x	x	x	x	LRS	CMP	
mallochi (Walley)	x	x	x	x	x	x	LRS	CIMP	
monilis (Linnaeus)		x		x	x		L	CP	
parajanta Roback	x	x	x	x	x	x	LRS	CIMP	
rhamphe Sublette		x	x	x	x	x	LR	CP	
simpsoni Roback					x		R	C	
undescribed species (5)									
(*Asayia*)									
annulata (Say)		x	x	x	x	x	LRS	CIP	
(*Karelia*)									
cinctipes (Johannsen)	x	x	x	x	x	x	LRS	CIMP	
idei (Walley)					x		L	CP	
illinoensis (Malloch)		x		x	x			CP	

Table 1. *Continued.*

Genus, subgenus, species, and author	AL	FL	GA	NC	SC	TN	Habitat	Region	Reference[b]
	State[a]								
peleensis (Walley)	x	x	x	x	x	x	LRS	CIP	
philosphagnos Beck and Beck		x	x	x			L	C	
undescribed species (3)									
Alotanypus									20
aris (Roback)	x			x			Sp	CM	
Apsectrotanypus									9
johnsoni (Coquillett)		x	x	x	x		LS	CM	
Bethbilbeckia									3
floridensis Fittkau and Murray		x	x		x		S	CM	
Brundiniella									9
eumorpha (Sublette)			x	x	x		SSp	MP	
Cantopelopia									5
gesta Roback		x	x		x			C	
Clinotanypus									7
aureus Roback		x					S	C	
pinguis (Loew)	x	x	x	x	x	x	LRSSp	CIMP	
planus Roback		x						C	
wirthi Roback		x						C	
Coelotanypus									6
concinnus (Coquillett)	x	x	x	x	x	x	LRS	CIP	
scapularis (Loew)	x	x	x	x	x	x	LRS	CIP	
tricolor (Loew)	x	x	x	x	x	x	LR	CIP	
Conchapelopia									12
aleta Roback			x	x	x	x	S	CMP	
fasciata Beck and Beck	x	x	x	x	x	x	S	CIMP	
pallens (Coquillett)		x		x	x		LRS	CMP	
rurika (Roback)	x		x	x	x	x	RSSp	CIMP	
Denopelopia									21
atria (Roback and Rutter)		x					S	C	
Djalmabatista									22
pulcher (Johannsen)	x	x	x	x	x	x	LRS	CIP	
Fittkauimyia									13
serta (Roback)		x						C	
sp. 2 Roback		x					LS	C	
Guttipelopia									1
guttipennis (v.d. Wulp)		x	x	x	x	x	LR	CMP	
Hayesomyia									4
senata (Walley)	x	x	x	x	x	x	R	CIMP	
Helopelopia									12
cornuticaudata (Walley)	x	x		x	x	x	RS	CIMP	
pilicaudata (Walley)				x				C	
Hudsonimyia									10
karelena Roback			x		x		Sp	M	
parrishi Caldwell and Soponis			x				Sp	P	
Krenopelopia									14
hudsoni Roback	x		x	x	x	x	SSp	IMP	
Labrundinia									19
becki Roback		x	x	x	x	x	LRS	CMP	

Table 1. *Continued.*

Genus, subgenus, species, and author	AL	FL	GA	NC	SC	TN	Habitat	Region	Reference[b]
			State[a]						
johannseni Beck and Beck	x	x	x	x		x	LRS	CIP	
maculata Roback				x			L	P	
neopilosella Beck and Beck	x	x	x	x	x	x	LR	CIMP	
pilosella (Loew)	x	x	x	x	x	x	RSSp	CIMP	
virescens Beck and Beck		x	x	x			LS	C	
sp. 3 nr. *virescens*				x			L	P	
sp. 4 sensu Roback	x	x		x	x		LRS	CP	
sp. 6 sensu Roback		x	x	x		x	LS	CI	
sp. 10 sensu Roback			x				RS	C	
undescribed species (3)									
Larsia									5
berneri Beck and Beck		x		x		x	LS	CI	
canadensis Bilyj					x			C	
decolorata (Malloch)		x	x	x	x	x	LS	CI	
planensis (Johannsen)					x		L	C	
undescribed species (1)									
Meropelopia									12
americana Fittkau		x	x	x	x	x	LS	CM	
flavifrons (Johannsen)		x	x	x	x	x	RSSp	CIMP	
Monopelopia									16
boliekae Beck and Beck		x	x				L	C	
tenuicalcar (Kieffer)		x					L	C	
tillandsia Beck and Beck		x					L	C	
undescribed species (1)									
Natarsia									9
baltimoreus (Macquart)	x	x	x	x	x	x	LS	CIMP	
sp. A. sensu Roback		x	x	x	x		S	CP	
Nilotanypus									17
americanus Beck and Beck		x	x	x	x		RS	CMP	
fimbriatus (Walker)	x	x	x	x	x		RS	CMP	
Paramerina									5
anomala Beck and Beck	x	x	x	x			S	C	
fragilis (Walley)					x			C	
undescribed species (1)									
Pentaneura									5
inconspicua (Malloch)	x	x	x		x		RS	CMP	
undescribed species (1)									
Procladius									11
(*Holotanypus*)									
curtus Roback		x						C	
denticulatus Sublette	x		x		x		L	C	
freemani Sublette		x	x	x	x		L	C	
sublettei Roback	x	x	x	x	x	x	LRS	CIMP	
wilhmi Roback						x	Sp	I	
(*Psilotanypus*)									
bellus (Loew)	x	x	x	x	x	x	LRS	CIMP	
undescribed species (2)									
Psectrotanypus									9
dyari (Coquillett)	x	x	x	x	x	x	RSSp	CIMP	

Table 1. *Continued.*

Genus, subgenus, species, and author	AL	FL	GA	NC	SC	TN	Habitat	Region	Reference[b]
undescribed species (1)									
Reomyia									18
undescribed species (1)			x				S	M	
Rheopelopia									12
acra (Roback)			x	x	x		S	M	
perda (Roback)			x				S	P	
sp. 2 sensu Roback			x				R	C	
sp. 3 sensu Roback			x	x			S	M	
Tanypus									8
(*Apelopia*)									
clavatus Beck	x	x					L	C	
neopunctipennis Sublette	x	x	x	x	x	x	LRSSp	CIMP	
(*Tanypus*)									
carinatus Sublette		x	x	x	x	x	LRSSp	CMP	
punctipennis Meigen	x	x	x	x	x		LRS	CP	
stellatus Coquillett		x	x	x	x	x	LR	CIP	
telus Roback		x						C	
Thienemannimyia									12
undescribed species (1)	x						S	P	
Trissopelopia									2
ogemawi Roback			x	x	x		RS	P	
Zavrelimyia									5
bifasciata (Coquillett)					x			P	
sinuosa (Coquillett)	x		x	x	x	x	SSp	CIMP	
thryptica (Sublette)			x		x			CP	
Undescribed Genus I					x			C	See text

[a] States: AL, Alabama; FL, Florida; GA, Georgia; NC, North Carolina; SC, South Carolina; TN, Tennessee.

[b] References: (1) Bilyj 1988; (2) Caldwell 1984; (3) Fittkau and Murray 1988; (4) Murray and Fittkau 1985; (5) Roback 1971; (6) Roback 1974; (7) Roback 1976; (8) Roback 1977; (9) Roback 1978; (10) Roback 1979; (11) Roback 1980; (12) Roback 1981; (13) Roback 1982b; (14) Roback 1983; (15) Roback 1985; (16) Roback 1986a; (17) Roback 1986b; (18) Roback 1986c; (19) Roback 1987a; (20) Roback 1987b; (21) Roback and Rutter 1988; (22) Roback and Tennessen 1978.

for example, *Paraboreochlus* (Table 2)—only the genus name is listed. If generic records are based on adults, no described species are present, and the adults appear new to science, we use the "undescribed species" listing—for example, *Krenosmittia* (Table 3). State distribution by species is still incomplete, since most systematic State collections are based on immature forms. In well-known genera (e.g., *Ablabesmyia*), or monotypic genera, the distribution within the region can be established. For most genera—for example, *Eukiefferiella* of the Orthocladiinae (Table 3), with several undescribed species and collections of adults only—the distribution at the species level is incomplete. In the Tables, this situation suggests that many genera have only a limited distribution, when in fact they are widely distributed but collections have been based only on immatures. Larval taxonomy has become sufficiently developed to at least estimate the diversity within a genus group. These estimates were used, along with adult collections, to estimate the number of undescribed species in the Southeast within a given genus.

Habitat designations are somewhat broad but should help establish general preferences. The distinction between lotic and lentic habitats is unclear in the coastal plains, where creeks and rivers are usually associated with swamps. The predominance of lotic habitat designations in upland areas may in part reflect the rarity of natural lentic habitat in the Southeast and the propensity for environmental monitoring agencies to focus on streams and rivers. Also, many of the adult

Table 2. *Summary of distribution and habitat for Podonominae, Telmatogetoninae, Diamesinae, and Prodiamesinae in the southeastern United States. Habitat: L = lakes (natural, impoundments, swamps), M = marine, R = river (> 12 m wide), S = streams (≤ 12 m wide), Sp = seeps or springs, T = terrestrial. Regions (see Figure for locations): C = Coastal Plain including Sandhills, I = Interior Upland, M = Mountains (Ridge and Valley and Appalachian), P = Piedmont Plateau.*

Genus, subgenus, species, and author	State[a]						Habitat	Region	Reference[b]
	AL	FL	GA	NC	SC	TN			
Podonominae									
Boreochlus									9
persimilis Johannsen					x			M	
Paraboreochlus				x			S	M	1
Telmatogetoninae									
Telmatogeton									8
japonicus Tokunaga		x	x				M	C	
Thalassomya									8
bureni Wirth		x					M	C	
Diamesinae									
Diamesa									2
nivoriunda (Fitch)	x		x	x	x	x	S	IMP	
undescribed species (3+)									
Pagastia									5
orthogonia Oliver				x		x	RSSp	M	
Potthastia									3
iberica Serra-Tosio			x				S	M	
longimana Kieffer	x	x	x	x	x	x	RS	CIMP	
gaedii (Meigen)			x	x			RS	MP	
Sympotthastia									4
zavreli (Pagast)				x			S	MP	
Undescribed genus	x	x	x	x			S	C	3
(= Genus P sensu Doughman)									
Prodiamesinae									
Compteromesa									6
oconeensis Saether					x			P	
Odontomesa									7
fulva nearctica Saether			x	x	x		S	CMP	
Prodiamesa									6
olivacea Meigen			x	x	x		S	CMP	

[a] States: AL, Alabama; FL, Florida; GA, Georgia; NC, North Carolina; SC, South Carolina; TN, Tennessee.
[b] References: (1) Coffman et al. 1988; (2) Doughman 1983; (3) Doughman 1985a; (4) Doughman 1985b; (5) Oliver and Roussel 1982; (6) Saether 1985e; (7) Saether 1985g; (8) Wirth 1952; (9) Wirth and Sublette 1970.

collections include immatures whose habitat is somewhere in the continuum from the shoreline to the uplands; chironomid genera with unusual larval habitats were listed by Hudson (1987). For the aquatic species collected only as adults, no designation of habitat is given, even though it may be well established elsewhere; such determinations are clearly needed for the Southeast. The division between streams and rivers was based on a frequency plot of widths in Roback's (1976) description of sampling stations in the East. There was a sharp break in width frequency near 12 m; consequently we make a tentative distinction between streams and rivers in the Southeast at this 12-m width.

The southeastern States included here contain at least four physiographic provinces or regions: the coastal plain, piedmont, mountain, and interior uplands (Figure). Florida is entirely within the coastal plain; in North Carolina, South Carolina, Georgia, and Alabama, this habitat extends from the Atlantic and Gulf coasts to the fall line. We also consider the area west

Table 3. *Summary of distribution and habitat for Orthocladiinae in the southeastern United States. Habitat: L = lakes (natural, impoundments, swamps), M = marine, R = river (>12 m wide), S = streams (≤12 m wide), Sp = seeps or springs, T = terrestrial. Regions (see Figure for locations): C = Coastal Plain including Sandhills, I = Interior Upland, M = Mountains (Ridge and Valley and Appalachian), P = Piedmont Plateau.*

Genus, subgenus, species, and author	State[a]						Habitat	Region	Reference[b]
	AL	FL	GA	NC	SC	TN			
Acricotopus					x			P	8
Antillocladius									29
arcuatus Saether					x		S	MP	
pluspilalus Saether			x		x			CMP	
Apometriocnemus									31
fontinalis Saether						x		M	
Brillia									19
flavifrons (Johannsen)	x	x	x	x	x		S	CMP	
parva Johannsen				x			S	M	
sera Roback	x		x	x	x		S	CMP	
undescribed species (2)									
Bryophaenocladius									27
digitatus Saether					x		T	P	
fumosinus (Curran)					x		T	C	
impectinus Saether					x		T	M	
psilacrus Saether					x		T	C	
undescribed species (6+)									
Camptocladius									9
stercorarius (DeGeer)			x				T	P	
Cardiocladius									18
albiplumus Saether			x	x		x	S	IMP	
obscurus (Johannsen)		x		x	x			CP	
undescribed species (3+)									
Chaetocladius									21
stamfordi (Johannsen)			x	x	x		SSp	CIP	
undescribed sepcies (3+)									
Chasmatonotus									20
bicolor Rempel						x	T	M	
bimaculatus Ost. Saken						x	T	M	
unimaculatus Loew				x			T	M	
undescribed species (2+)									
Clunio									42
marshalli Stone and Wirth		x					M	C	
Compterosmittia									27
nerius (Curran)					x		T	CP	
Corynoneura									2
fittkaui Lehman			x		x		L	P	
lacustris (Walley)					x			C	
lobata Edwards					x		S	CP	
scutellata Winnertz		x						C	
taris Roback	x	x	x		x		RS	C	
undescribed species (2+)									
Cricotopus									15
(*Cricotopus*)									
albiforceps Kieffer			x				L	P	

Table 3. *Continued.*

| Genus, subgenus, species, and author | State[a] | | | | | | Habitat | Region | Reference[b] |
	AL	FL	GA	NC	SC	TN			
annulator Goetghebuer					x		LRS	MP	
bicinctus (Meigen)	x	x	x	x	x	x	LRS	CP	
coronatus Hirvenoja				x				P	
festivellus (Kieffer)				x			L	P	
luciae LeSage and Harrison				x	x			P	
politus (Coquillett)		x					S	C	
slossonae (Malloch)				x	x		LS	P	
tremulus (Linnaeus)			x				S	P	
trifascia Edwards		x		x			S	P	
triannulatus (Macquart)				x	x		R	P	
varipes Coquillett		x		x	x		LRS	CP	
vierriensis Goetghebuer	x	x		x	x	x		CP	
(*Isocladius*)									
sylvestris (Fabricius)				x	x		LRS	P	
trifasciatus (Meigen)		x		x	x		LRS	CP	
(*Nostococladius*)									
nostocicola Wirth			x	x	x		S	M	
(subgenus unknown)									
belkini Dendy and Sublette	x						L	P	
undescribed species (10+)									
Diplocladius									27
cultriger Kieffer	x		x	x	x		LS	CMP	
Diplosmittia									35
carinata Saether			x				T	P	
Doithrix									39
parcivillosa Saether and Sublette					x		Sp	M	
villosa Saether and Sublette					x	x	Sp	MP	
Doncricotopus		x	x				R	CP	25
Epoicocladius									21
flavens (Malloch)			x	x		x	LRS	IMP	
undescribed species (2)									
Eukiefferiella									1
brehmi Gowin				x	x		S	M	
brevicalcar (Kieffer)					x		R	P	
brevinervis (Malloch)					x			C	
coerulescens (Kieffer)					x		R	MP	
claripennis (Lundbeck)				x	x		RS	M	
devonica (Edwards)			x		x			M	
ilkleyensis (Edwards)				x	x		R	P	
lobifera (Goetghebuer)					x			P	
undescribed species (7+)									
Euryhapsis				x		x		M	16
Georthocladius									27
(*Georthocladius*)									
fimbriosus Saether and Sublette					x	x	Sp	M	
triquetrus Saether and Sublette					x		Sp	P	
(*Atelopodella*)									
curticornus Saether				x	x		ST	M	

Table 3. *Continued.*

Genus, subgenus, species, and author	AL	FL	GA	NC	SC	TN	Habitat	Region	Reference[b]
Gymnometriocnemus									28
(*Gymnometriocnemus*)									
subnudus (Edwards)				x		x		MP	
(*Raphidocladius*)									
brumalis (Edwards)				x	x	x	SSp	M	
Heleniella									30
hirta Saether			x	x			S	M	
parva Saether					x	x	SSp	MP	
Heterotrissocladius									22
marcidus (Walker)		x	x	x	x		S	CM	
sp. C sensu Saether		x		x			S	C	
undescribed species (2)									
Hydrobaenus									23
johannseni (Sublette)				x	x		L	P	
pilipes (Malloch)		x	x				RS	C	
pilipodex Saether	x						S	I	
undescribed species (1+)									
Krenosmittia									11
undescribed species (2)				x			S	MP	
Limnophyes									8, 37
asquamatus (Anderson)				x				C	
borealis (Holmgren)				x	x			MP	
carolinensis Saether				x	x			MP	
fumosus Johannsen			x		x		S	MP	
pumilio (Holmgren)			x	x				M	
minimus (Meigen)		x	x	x	x	x	LS	CMP	
Lipurometriocnemus									27
vixlobatus Saether			x	x	x			CP	
c.f. glabalus Saether			x					C	
Lopescladius									7
(*Cordiella*)									
hyporheicus (Coffman and Roback)				x				C	
(subgenus unknown)									
sp. 1 sensu Coffman and Roback				x			R	C	
undescribed species (1)									
Mesocricotopus									6
undescribed species (1)			x						
Mesosmittia									32
mina Saether			x					P	
patrihortae Saether			x		x			CP	
prolixa Saether			x			x		MP	
Metriocnemus									36
fuscipes (Meigen)			x	x	x	x	S	CM	
knabi Coquillett		x		x			T	CM	
obscuripes (Holmgren)				x	x			M	
Nanocladius									24
(*Nanocladius*)									
alternantherae (Dendy and Sublette)	x			x	x		L	P	

Table 3. *Continued.*

Genus, subgenus, species, and author	State[a]						Habitat	Region	Reference[b]
	AL	FL	GA	NC	SC	TN			
balticus (Palmen)				x	x		R	P	
crassicornus Saether	x	x	x		x	x	R	CI	
distinctus (Malloch)	x	x	x	x	x	x	LRS	CMP	
incomptus Saether			x	x	x		LS	P	
minimus Saether	x	x	x	x	x		LR	CMP	
parvulus (Kieffer)					x		S	C	
rectinervis (Kieffer)	x	x	x	x	x		LRS	CIMP	
spiniplenus Saether	x	x	x	x	x		LRS	CMP	
undescribed species (2)									
(*Plecopteracoluthus*)									
c.f. *branchicolus* Saether			x				S	M	
downesi (Steffan)			x	x	x		S	MP	
undescribed species (1)									
Oliveridia									12
undescribed species (2)				x			S	CP	
Orthocladius									40
(*Eudactylocladius*)									
dubitatus Johannsen			x	x			S	MP	
(*Euorthocladius*)									
rivicola Kieffer			x	x			S	M	
thienemanni Kieffer			x		x		S	MP	
(*Orthocladius*)									
annectens Saether		x	x		x			C	
carlatus (Roback)	x		x	x	x	x	RS	CIMP	
curtiseta Saether					x			C	
dentifer Brundin					x		R	CP	
dorenus (Roback)				x				CMP	
mallochi Kieffer					x		R	P	
nigritus Malloch				x	x		S	MP	
obumbratus Johannsen	x		x	x	x		RS	CMP	
oliveri Soponis	x			x				CI	
robacki Soponis				x				MP	
subletti Soponis					x			C	
(*Symposiocladius*)									
lignicola (Kieffer)	x	x	x	x	x	x	RS	CIMP	
undescribed species (6)									
Parachaetocladius									39
abnobaeus (Wulker)		x	x	x	x	x	SSp	CMP	
sp. B sensu Saether and Sublette					x		S	M	
Paracricotopus									4
glaber Saether	x		x	x	x		SSp	M	
millrockensis Caldwell			x	x	x		S	CMP	
mozleyi Steiner			x				S	M	
Parakiefferiella									21
coronata (Edwards)			x	x	x		LR	CP	
undescribed species (5+)									
Parametriocnemus									21
hamatus (Johannsen)					x			CM	
lundbecki (Johannsen)	x	x	x	x	x		S	CMP	

Table 3. *Continued.*

Genus, subgenus, species, and author	AL	FL	GA	NC	SC	TN	Habitat	Region	Reference[b]
					State[a]				
cf. *vespertinus* Saether			x				S	M	
undescribed species (4)									26
Paraphaenocladius									
exagitans Johannsen				x				CP	
nasthecus Saether				x				C	
undescribed species (1+)									9
Paratrichocladius									
rufiventris (Meigen)				x				M	
undescribed species (2)									27
Platysmittia									
fimbriata Saether					x			M	27
Plhudsonia									
partita Saether					x		Sp	M	21
Psectrocladius									
(*Allopsectrocladius*)			x	x	x		LRS	CMP	
(*Mesopsectrocladius*)			x				S	P	
(*Monopsectrocladius*)			x	x			S	CM	
(*Psectrocladius*)									
elatus Roback									
limbatellus (Holmgren) grp.									
cf. *octomaculatus* Walker			x					CP	
psilopterus Kieffer grp.			x		x			CP	
simulans (Johannsen)		x		x	x			CP	
vernalis (Malloch)	x	x		x	x		L	CP	
undescribed species (2+)									39
Pseudorthocladius									
(*Lordella*)									
wingoi Saether and Sublette				x	x			CMP	
(*Pseudorthocladius*)									
amplicaudus Saether and Sublette					x			C	
clavatosus Saether and Sublette					x			P	
curticornis Saether and Sublette					x	x	Sp	M	
destitutus Saether and Sublette					x			C	
dumicaudus Saether					x			C	
macrostomus Soponis		x						CP	
macrovirgatus Saether and Sublette				x		x		C	
morsei Saether and Sublette			x		x			MP	
paravirgatus Saether and Sublette				x	x			M	
rectilobus Saether and Sublette			x					CP	
tricanthus Saether and Sublette							Sp	CM	
uniserratus Saether and Sublette					x	x	Sp	CMP	
virgatus Saether and Sublette						x	Sp	M	
sp. A sensu Saether and Sublette					x		Sp	P	
sp. B sensu Saether and Sublette							Sp		
undescribed species (1+)									8
Pseudosmittia									
digitata Saether		x	x					CP	
forcipata (Goetgh.)		x	x	x	x		T	CMP	
cf. *mathildae* Albu			x					P	

Table 3. *Continued.*

Genus, subgenus, species, and author	State[a]						Habitat	Region	Reference[b]
	AL	FL	GA	NC	SC	TN			
nanseni (Kieffer)			x					P	
undescribed species (4+)									
Psilometriocnemus									27
triannulatus Saether			x	x	x	x	Sp	MP	
Rheocricotopus									33
(*Psilocricotopus*)									
conflusirus Saether					x			M	
glabricollis (Meigen)				x	x	x	S	MP	
robacki (Beck and Beck)	x	x	x	x	x	x	SSp	CIMP	
(*Rheocricotopus*)									
amplicristatus Saether					x			C	
effusus (Walker)				x	x		SSp	P	
eminellobus Saether				x	x	x	SSp	CMP	
pauciseta Saether				x			S	M	
tuberculatus Caldwell		x	x	x	x	x	SSp	CIMP	
Rheosmittia									10
spinicornis (Brundin)				x	x		L	P	
undescribed species (2+)									
Saetheriella									13
amplicristata Halvorsen					x			M	
Smittia									26
aterrima (Malloch)		x	x	x	x		T	CMP	
lasiops (Malloch)		x						C	
undescribed species (4+)									
Stilocladius									27
clinopecten Saether			x	x	x		RS	CM	
Sublettiella									28
calvata Saether					x			CM	
Symbiocladius									3
(*Symbiocladius*)									
chattahoocheensis Caldwell			x				S	M	
equitans (Classen)				x			S	M	
Synorthocladius									9
semivirens (Kieffer)	x		x	x	x	x	RS	CIMP	
undescribed species (1)									
Thienemannia									34
pilinucha Saether						x		M	
Thienemanniella									2
obscura Brundin					x			P	
partita Schlee					x		SC		
xena (Roback)		x	x	x	x		S	CP	
undescribed species (2+)									
Tokunagaia				x			SSp	M	14
Tvetenia									38, 1
bavarica (Thienemann)				x	x			P	
calvescens (Edwards)			x				RS	P	
paucunca (Saether)			x	x	x			CMP	
veralli (Edwards)				x			R	P	

Table 3. *Continued.*

Genus, subgenus, species, and author	State[a]						Habitat	Region	Reference[b]
	AL	FL	GA	NC	SC	TN			
vitracies (Saether)				x	x			CP	
Unniella									5
multivirga Saether		x	x	x	x		RS	C	
Xylotopus									17
par (Coquillet)	x	x	x	x	x	x	LRS	CMP	
Zalutschia									41
briani Soponis		x		x	x		LRS	C	
zalutchicola (Lipina)			x	x	x		L	P	
undescribed species (2)									
Genus near *Georthocladius*						x	Sp	M	39
Orthocladiinae sp. A					x		S	M	27
Orthocladiinae sp. B					x		S	P	27
Orthocladiinae sp. C		x			x	x	LS	C	27

[a] States: AL, Alabama; FL, Florida; GA, Georgia; NC, North Carolina; SC, South Carolina; TN, Tennessee.
[b] References: (1) Bode 1983; (2) Boesel and Winner 1980; (3) Caldwell 1984; (4) Caldwell 1985; (5) Caldwell 1986; (6) Coffman et al. 1986; (7) Coffman and Roback 1984; (8) Cranston and Oliver 1988a; (9) Cranston et al. 1983; (10) Cranston and Saether 1986; (11) Ferrington 1984; (12) Ferrington and Saether 1987; (13) Halvorsen 1982; (14) Halvorsen and Saether 1987; (15) LeSage and Harrison 1980; (16) Oliver 1981; (17) Oliver 1985; (18) Oliver and Bode 1985; (19) Oliver and Roussel 1983; (20) Rempel 1937; (21) Saether 1969; (22) Saether 1975a; (23) Saether 1976; (24) Saether 1977b; (25) Saether 1981a; (26) Saether 1981b; (27) Saether 1982 ; (28) Saether 1983a; (29) Saether 1984; (30) Saether 1985a; (31) Saether 1985b; (32) Saether 1985c; (33) Saether 1985d; (34) Saether 1985f; (35) Saether 1985h; (36) Saether 1989; (37) Saether 1990; (38) Saether and Halvorsen 1981; (39) Saether and Sublette 1983; (40) Soponis 1977; (41) Soponis 1979; (42) Wirth 1952.

Figure. Major physiographic regions of the southeastern United States.

of the Tennessee River in Tennessee to be coastal plain. The piedmont occupies the area between the fall line and the foot of the mountains to the west and north in North Carolina, South Carolina, Georgia, and Alabama. The mountains are the Appalachian Highlands, including the ridge and valley section. What we call the interior uplands consists of the Cumberland Plateau, Highland Rim Plateau, and other upland areas west to the Tennessee River; a small section is in Georgia (uncollected), a larger portion in Alabama, and most in central Tennessee. The coastal plain lies between sea level and about 150 m above mean sea level, the piedmont between 150 and 300 m, the mountains above 300 m, and the interior uplands from 150 to 600 m.

The references cited represent the most current or comprehensive treatment of each genus known to us. Most contain additional sources for further research. Wiederholm (1983, 1986) and Brigham et al. (1982) should also be consulted for overall reviews and summaries.

For each subfamily or group of subfamilies, we provide brief descriptions of key characteristics of the genera or of unique species in the genera. For the large and taxonomically difficult genera we use the term species group. These are assemblages of closely related species within a genus and the term provides a convenient way to discuss these genera. The format is not rigidly structured or entirely uniform in each instance, because the information available for each species or genus varies widely. We have tried not to duplicate the information on ecology and distribution in the Holarctic keys of Wiederholm (1983, 1986), but provide our own observations on biological or taxonomic problems that have vexed us.

Tanypodinae

The Tanypodinae (Table 1) occurs in a wide variety of habitats in the Southeast. Our collections indicated a relatively even distribution between lakes, streams, and rivers. The estimates have not been weighted by area or intensity of collection. About 10% of the species were collected from unusual habitats that we listed under springs and seeps—hygropetric areas, banks, floodplains, other animals (symbiotic relations), and water held in plants (Hudson 1987). Substantially more species of Tanypodinae occur in the coastal plain (77) than in the piedmont (52) or the mountains (37). The few species (30) recorded from the interior upland partly reflect the paucity of collections. The number of species per State also reflects sampling intensity; the largest numbers (58-62) were collected in Florida, Georgia, North Carolina, and South Carolina.

We identified 34 genera of Tanypodinae from the Southeast, of which only 1 is undescribed. Of the 109 species, 80 (73%) are described, and 8 of the 29 undescribed larvae and pupae are illustrated in various publications. The largest numbers of species are in *Ablabesmyia* (22) and *Labrundinia* (13); in contrast, 23 genera in the Southeast contain only 1 or 2 known species. We next describe some of the characteristics of each of the 34 genera listed in Table 1.

Ablabesmyia. This genus is common and widespread in the Southeast; 14 of the 15 described Nearctic species occur in this region. The diversity of species is greatest in the coastal plain or piedmont areas; routine collections in these areas usually yield two or three species per site. In streams (where sampling has been most intense), the two most common species are *A. mallochi* and *A. parajanta*, both of which tolerate pollution well. *Ablabesmyia idei* and *A. monilis* have been collected in reservoirs and *A. philosphagnos* in swamps. More unusual

habitats have been recorded for *A. janta*, which occurs symbiotically in mussels (Roback 1982a), and *A. peleensis*, which has been collected from the axils of bromeliads.

The use of species keys given by Roback (1985) is essential for the identifications of immature stages; however, he notes that their identifications can be difficult. There have been many changes and synonymies; for example, *A. ornata* and *A. tarella* have been synonymized with *A. mallochi*. The immature stages of *A. cinctipes* are not included in Roback's (1985) review; however, the pupa has been described by Beck and Beck (1966) and the larva was keyed by Beck (1976) but never formally described. As judged by the numerous varieties listed by Roback (1985), and by our own observations, there may be as many as eight undescribed species in the Southeast.

Ablabesmyia larvae in alcohol often can be separated from other genera by gross morphology (presence of darkened claws on the posterior prolegs, lateral bulging of the head capsule) and pigmentation (blotched with red or purple). Larvae of *A. annulata* are easily recognized by their long procercus (length–width ratio about 7 to 8; less than 4 in other species).

Alotanypus. Collections of the only known species in this genus, *A. aris*, are rare in the Southeast. The only two records consist of an adult from North Carolina and a complete rearing (emerging adult with associated exuviae) from a spring in Alabama. The rarity may be partly accounted for by the infrequently sampled habitat (seeps) and the unavailability of descriptions of larval characteristics until the late 1970's (Roback 1978). *Alotanypus* was considered a subgenus of *Macropelopia* by Roback (1978).

Apsectrotanypus. The single species in the Southeast, *A. johnsoni*, has had other generic names in the past (*Macropelopia*, *Psectrotanypus*). It is most commonly collected in small mountain streams, although it has been reported in the coastal plains. This genus will probably also be found in the piedmont.

Bethbilbeckia. This genus was described by Fittkau and Murray (1988) in all stages except the female. The genus is equivalent to Tanypodinae Genus I of Fittkau and Murray (1986), who described the pupal stage. The type specimens were collected from a black water stream (having high concentrations of particulate and dissolved organic matter) in northeastern Florida. The species has been collected in Georgia from a seep area in leaf litter.

C. N. Watson (personal communication) has reared a female of this genus from a small stream in the mountains of South Carolina. The larva is pale red.

Brundiniella. The single species in the Southeast, *B. eumorpha*, has had several generic names (*Anatopynia*, *Brundinia*, *Psectrotanypus*). It is common in small mountain and upper piedmont streams. Gut contents usually include large sand grains, suggesting that the larva feeds by grazing.

Cantopelopia. Because the immature stages of *C. gesta* are unknown, Hudson (1987) speculated that they may be terrestrial or semiterrestrial. Among the records known for the Southeast are adults from the Savannah River Plant of the U.S. Department of Energy in South Carolina, and a small Georgia black water stream on the coastal plain. B. Bilyj (personal communication) has examined and verified *C. gesta* specimens from Florida in the Beck collection.

Clinotanypus. The species *C. pinguis* is widespread in the Southeast, occurring in a variety of aquatic habitats having soft sediments. It seems to prefer smaller and shallower bodies of water than *Coelotanypus* (Roback 1976)—particularly the near-bank areas of slow-moving streams. The other three species listed are known only from Florida, and two of them only in the adult stage.

Coelotanypus. All three species of this genus share the same basic distribution and habitat and lack distinctive morphological characters—suggesting a single variable species. Morphologically similar species of *Clinotanypus* were synonymized by Roback (1971). Although *Coelotanypus* is fairly widespread, it has not been collected in the mountains. *Coelotanypus concinnus* is the most common of the three species in North Carolina. Larvae of all southeastern *Coelotanypus* can be identified by a pair of brown chitinized processes on the first abdominal segment. This character is useful in sorting larvae in alcohol.

Conchapelopia. Several species formerly in this genus are now in *Helopelopia* and *Meropelopia* (Roback 1981), and Bilyj (1985) established several synonymies within the genus. *Conchapelopia* in the Southeast can be separated in the pupal stage, but available larval characteristics definitively separate only *C. rurika* from the rest. *Conchapelopia* is a member of the *Thienemannimyia* group of genera (Murray and Fittkau 1985) and the long scattered body setae in this group quickly separate larvae of *Conchapelopia* and other members of the group. *Conchapelopia* species are more common in the mountains than in the coastal plain (Roback 1981); they are most often found in flowing water, and some species (usually identified as "*Conchapelopia* group") are very tolerant of chemical and organic pollution. Caldwell (1984) collected *C. aleta* in aquatic moss, leaf litter, and decomposing vegetation in a second-order stream. R. P. Rutter (personal communication) has collected specimens of *Conchapelopia* from the littoral zone of an oligotrophic lake in south-central Florida.

Denopelopia. This recently erected monotypic genus was described in all stages by Roback and Rutter (1988). It is known only from the type locality, a drainage ditch choked with cattails (*Typha* sp.) in southwestern Florida. The larvae of *D. atria* are tolerant of extended periods of low dissolved oxygen and relatively high iron concentrations; they feed on chironomid larvae, naidids, ploimate rotifers, and diatoms.

Djalmabatista. One species, *D. pulcher*, appears to be widely distributed in the nonmountainous areas of the Southeast. In North Carolina it occurs in both lakes and slow-moving coastal plain streams and rivers. Tennessen and Gottfried (1983) have found much variation in the number and shape of teeth on the ligula of *Djalmabatista* from Alabama. The typical ligula has four teeth. The most common form of abnormal ligula has five symmetrical teeth, resembling the ligulae of *Procladius* and two South American species of *Djalmabatista*. *Djalmabatista* with both four- and five-toothed ligulae are known from Florida and North Carolina (R. P. Rutter and T. J. Wilda, personal communication).

Fittkauimyia. The single species, *F. serta*, was originally described by Roback (1971) from an adult collected in Florida, as belonging to a new genus, *Parapelopia*. This synonymy is still tentative (Roback 1982b), and specimens described as *Fittkauimyia* sp. 2 may be a new species and *Parapelopia* a legitimate genus. In Florida, D. L. Evans (personal communication) found *Fittkauimyia* primarily in shallow water with mixed emergent vegetation (particularly freshwater marshes).

Guttipelopia. Bilyj (1988), who provided a comprehensive review of geographic distribution, larval habitats, and phenologies, concluded that specimens of *G. currani* initially described from Florida and later identified from most southeastern States in fact represent a further range extension of *G. guttipennis*, which is a widely distributed Holarctic species. *Guttipelopia* is most common in the coastal plain.

Hayesomyia. The genus contains the single species *H. senata*, formerly placed in *Thienemannimyia* and the *Thienemannimyia* group of genera (Murray and Fittkau 1985). The pupa has a distinctive thoracic horn, similar to that in some species of *Thienemannimyia*. *Hayesomyia* is a characteristic Tanypodinae of large rivers in the Southeast and is widely distributed.

Helopelopia. This genus was formerly a subgenus of *Conchapelopia*. Although *Helopelopia cornuticaudata* is widespread, *H. pilicaudata* is known only from adults collected at the Savannah River Plant in South Carolina. *Helopelopia* is a member of the *Thienemannimyia* group of genera (Murray and Fittkau 1985).

Hudsonimyia. The two species of this genus inhabit similar hygropetric biotopes but may separate out geographically (mountain versus piedmont). *Hudsonimyia karelena* may also be a more voracious predator than *H. parrishi*. Certain aspects of coloration of the immature stages may not strictly conform to published descriptions (e.g., variation in color in some *H. karelena* may be greater than originally believed).

Krenopelopia. Several specimens have been collected in streams, but it may be assumed that they had washed in from their more typical spring-seep habitat (Roback 1983).

Labrundinia. Roback's (1987a) revision of the genus added four possible species to the fauna of the Southeast. R. P. Rutter (personal communication) found two additional types (with pustulate head and maculation) in Florida marshes. *Labrundinia neopilosella*, *L. pilosella*, and *L. virescens* are the most common and widespread *Labrundinia* in North Carolina. In general, they prefer slow water but are also found in backwater areas in many fast-flowing streams (Roback 1987a). *Labrundinia* sp. 4 is common in Mayo Reservoir, North Carolina, where it occurs in beds of bushy pondweed, *Najas guadalupensis* (B. H. Tracy, personal communication). Larvae of *Labrundinia* are usually smaller than those of the other Tanypodinae, except *Nilotanypus*.

Larsia. In North Carolina, species of *Larsia* occur primarily in lentic situations, but can also be found in slow-moving streams of the coastal plain. In Florida the larvae of *Larsia* are common in marshes. Roback (1971)

synonymized *L. lurida* and *L. indistincta* of Beck and Beck (1966) with *L. decolorata*. However, B. Bilyj (personal communication) believes that *L. indistincta* is a distinct species.

Meropelopia. This genus was a subgenus of *Arctopelopia* (Roback 1971) and *Conchapelopia* (Roback 1981) until it was elevated to the generic level by Fittkau and Roback (1983). It is a member of the *Thienemannimyia* group (Murray and Fittkau 1985). Identification of species is difficult, because the two known species separate only on the basis of size (Roback 1981). Caldwell (1984) collected *M. flavifrons* from leaf litter in a first-order stream in the mountains of northern Georgia. Some *Meropelopia* larvae appear to be rather tolerant of pollution.

Monopelopia. Larvae are relatively scarce and inhabit small bodies of water in the coastal plain. One of us (B.A.C.) has collected an undescribed species or what may prove to be a variant of *M. tenuicalcar* in small streams and standing water along the Georgia coastal plain. *Monopelopia tillandsia* has been collected only in water held in bromeliad axils; *M. boliekae* lives in shallow, weed-choked environments.

Natarsia. Members of the genus *Natarsia* are often associated with organic and toxic discharges, especially sewage, as a subdominant in the chironomid community. The unnamed "sp. A" (Roback 1978) is the more common of the two in North Carolina; it appears to be limited to the coastal plain and piedmont. In Georgia, *Natarsia* sp. A has been a subdominant in organically enriched piedmont streams. Larvae in alcohol can be easily identified by the cluster of four setae near the anterolateral or mediolateral margin of abdominal segments I–VII (Roback 1978).

Nilotanypus. Species of *Nilotanypus* are most commonly found in clear, relatively shallow (<2 m), sand- and gravel-bottomed streams with good to excellent water quality; however, two of the known species occur in the lower Savannah River, a large, silt-laden coastal plain river. Only *N. fimbriatus* is common and widespread.

Paramerina. Species of *Paramerina* are often confused with those of *Zavrelimyia*. The most common species is *P. anomala*, and (since no larval keys exist) benthologists have assumed it to be the sole representative in the Southeast. However, the record of *P. fragilis*, from an adult collected at the Savannah River Plant, makes that assumption dubious. R. P. Rutter (personal communication) found the genus to be common in marsh habitats in Florida. A larval description is available for *P. anomala* (Beck and Beck 1966).

Pentaneura. The undescribed species included in our checklist (Table 1) is represented by an adult collected at the Savannah River Plant. Roback (1971) synonymized *P. inculta* from Florida (Beck and Beck 1966) with *P. inconspicua*, which is basically a western species. Larvae of this genus are most abundant in the coastal plain. M. W. Heyn (personal communication) has reared *P. inconspicua* larvae from the bank moss of streams.

Procladius. The most widely distributed species in the Southeast are *P. bellus* and *P. sublettei*; in North Carolina they are also the most abundant. These two species are commonly found together in the same silt–clay habitat. C. N. Watson (personal communication) is convinced that *P. bellus* includes at least two species. He found the different larval phenotypes (small, 3-4 mm; large, 5-7 mm) coexisting in the littoral zone. He suspected that further work would yield evidence for restricting the name *bellus* to the small phenotype and resurrecting the name *riparius* for the larger one. *Procladius wilhmi* is known only from the type locality near Oak Ridge, Tennessee. Some species tolerate low concentrations of dissolved oxygen, often co-occurring with large numbers of *Chironomus*.

Psectrotanypus. Along with *Chironomus*, *P. dyari* is abundant in streams polluted by sewage. Unmounted larvae are often light green. C. N. Watson (personal communication) collected an undescribed species similar to *P. discolor* (Coquillett), which is common in the Northeast, from a small stream in the mountains of South Carolina. The larva has a distinctive dark marking, with scalloped margins, on the dorsal surface of the head capsule.

Reomyia. This genus was erected by Roback (1986c) to include *Zavrelimyia wartinbei* Roback. The pupal stage of this taxon was described by Fittkau and Murray (1986) as Tanypodinae Genus III. The larval stage is unknown. An undescribed species has been collected in North Carolina at the Coweeta Hydrologic Laboratory of the U.S. Forest Service.

Rheopelopia. Larvae of *Rheopelopia* have been found in small, fast-flowing streams in North Carolina and large rivers in Georgia. Head capsules of larvae are usually marked with dark pigment and can be reasonably well separated to species—except for *R. perda* and *R. acra*, which Roback (1981) suggested could be one variable species. The systematic position of *Rheopelopia* in the *Thienemannimyia* group of genera was discussed by Murray and Fittkau (1985).

Tanypus. Several species of *Tanypus* are widely distributed throughout the Southeast, and all occur in the coastal plain. The immatures are typically collected in lakes or depositional areas of streams and rivers. *Tanypus neopunctipennis* is tolerant of some organic pollution; *T. clavatus* occurs in brackish water.

Thienemannimyia. The only described southeastern species has been transferred to *Hayesomyia*, and the placement of the single undescribed species is uncertain. Roback (1981) indicated that this is primarily a northern genus. This genus and others in the *Thienemannimyia* group were discussed by Murray and Fittkau (1985).

Trissopelopia. The larva has been described as cold-stenothermic (Fittkau and Murray 1986), but its occurrence in Georgia and North Carolina does not clearly fit this description. Larval specimens from North Carolina also did not fit all key characteristics given by Fittkau and Murray (1986). A redescription of North American material seems desirable.

Zavrelimyia. Inasmuch as a larval key is not available, distributional data for the immatures are questionable. Only the pupal stage can be relied on in making species identifications. Even in the adult stages there seems to be some doubt about the true identities of *Z. thryptica* and *Z. sinuosa*, since both form complexes of two or more morphologically similar species (B. Bilyj, personal communication).

Undescribed Genus I. The only known representative of this genus is one adult specimen (near *Pentaneura*) collected at the Savannah River Plant in South Carolina.

Podonominae, Telmatogetoninae, Diamesinae, Prodiamesinae

These four subfamilies contain relatively few taxa and are generally restricted to marine habitats (Telmatogetoninae) or more northern latitudes. A total of 12 genera and 17 species are known from the Southeast (Table 2); one of the genera and at least four of the species are undescribed. The Podonominae is restricted to mountainous areas and the Telmatogetoninae to marine intertidal zones. The Diamesinae and Prodiamesinae are more widely distributed but limited to flowing water.

Podonominae

Boreochlus. The only confirmed species from the Southeast is *B. persimilis*, represented by adults from the mountains in South Carolina. *Boreochlus* larvae have been collected from moss in a spring in the piedmont of South Carolina by one of us (P. L. H.) and in leaf pack samples from mountainous streams at the Coweeta Hydrologic Laboratory (A. D. Huryn, personal communication).

Paraboreochlus. Coffman et al. (1988) described the pupa and adult and presumed larva of the only known Nearctic species of *Paraboreochlus.* Our records are those of Beck (1980), from a North Carolina stream.

Telmatogetoninae

Telmatogeton. Collections and reports on chironomids of the marine intertidal zone in the Southeast are rare. Our records are literature reports based on collections in the late 1940's and some recent collections in Georgia and Florida. J. H. Epler (personal communication) reported them to be common on rock jetties in early spring (March) in Panama City and Jacksonville, Florida.

Thalassomya. Distributional records are similar to those for *Telematogeton.* Wirth (1949) reported a preference for waters of reduced salinity near harbors and river mouths. J. H. Epler (personal communication) collected them from rock jetties in Key West, Florida.

Diamesinae

Diamesa. Only one verified species is recorded from the Southeast. However, most taxonomic experts for this group have concentrated their efforts in northern North America, particularly the Northwest. Larval identification is particularly difficult because the mentum becomes abraded in feeding, and adults have rarely been collected. Collections of larvae in North Carolina suggest at least three additional species. They are most common in the mountains, but are occasionally collected in the piedmont. The described species *D. nivoriunda* tolerates high turbidity and siltation.

Pagastia. The genus is widespread in mountain rivers in North Carolina. The lack of larval keys and the weak flying ability of the adults may combine to account for its rarity in other collections. Larvae of *Pagastia* were collected from a spring in the interior uplands of Tennessee by D. L. Evans (personal communication).

Potthastia. The three species are distinctive in the larval stage. *Potthastia longimana* is widespread throughout North Carolina; *P. gaedii* is found in the mountains and upper piedmont. The North American fauna of this genus is in need of revision.

Sympotthastia. We follow Doughman (1985b) in listing *S. zavrelia* from North Carolina, although the larval record has not been confirmed by comparison with other stages in the Southeast. Although these larvae key to *S. zavrelia*, the generic diagnosis published by Oliver (1983) stated that all congeners have ventromental plates.

Undescribed genus. Larvae live in sandy substrates. In North Carolina they have been collected at only two locations in the sandhills. The larvae are equivalent to what Beck (1976) misidentified as *Sympotthastia* and Doughman (1985a) designated as Genus P. The larvae may in fact be immatures of *Compteromesa* from the Prodiamesinae.

Prodiamesinae

Compteromesa. Collections have been limited to adults in the vicinity of seeps and small streams in the upper piedmont. The larva of the above undescribed genus of Diamesinae may be that of *Compteromesa.*

Odontomesa. This genus is widespread, and habitat includes some polluted urban streams in the upper piedmont. It is most common in sandy, lightly silted sediments of slow-flowing water.

Prodiamesa. The habitat of *Prodiamesa* is similar to that of *Odontomesa*; it is also widespread and moderately tolerant of pollution.

Orthocladiinae

Species of Orthocladiinae (Table 3) occur in all six major habitats in the Southeast: of the species with known habits, 1 is marine; at least 14 are terrestrial;

and 166 live in fresh water—23 in springs, 29 in lakes, 35 in rivers, and 79 in streams. Orthoclads are rather evenly distributed (91–110 species) throughout the coastal plain, piedmont, and mountains; however, few have been recorded from the interior uplands—presumably due at least partly to lack of collecting effort. The most species (129) are known from South Carolina, where adults have been extensively collected.

We have identified 66 genera (Table 3); of these, 4 are undescribed but are represented in various publications by illustrations of at least one immature stage. *Cricotopus* (27 species) and *Orthocladius* (21 species) are the most diverse. Other relatively large genera (more than 10 species each) are *Bryophaenocladius*, *Eukiefferiella*, *Psectrocladius*, *Pseudorthocladius*, and *Nanocladius*. Most of the genera contain only one to three species in the Southeast. We have listed 275 species, of which 94 are undescribed; the immature stages of only 9 of these have been illustrated.

Acricotopus. The only representative of this genus is a pupa collected from the mouth of a small stream entering Keowee Reservoir, South Carolina. Cranston and Oliver (1988a) have synonymized *A. senex* with *A. nitidellus*.

Antillocladius. The immature stages for one species (*A. arcuatus*) are known from seep areas and stream margins.

Apometriocnemus. The immature stages are unknown for the single species described, *A. fontinalis*. The preferred habitat is probably semiterrestrial.

Brillia. The revision of Nearctic species by Oliver and Roussel (1983) must be consulted for species determinations. Two species groups are recognized—*flavifrons* (*flavifrons* and *sera*) and *modesta* (*parva*). In general, larvae of the *flavifrons* group mine in wood and those of the *modesta* group feed on leaves (Oliver and Roussel 1983).

Bryophaenocladius. The immature stages are believed to be primarily terrestrial. All southeastern species records are based on adults. An occasional larva has been found in streams and rivers in North Carolina. As judged by males collected, several—perhaps six—undescribed species occur in the Southeast.

Camptocladius. The sole species in the genus, *C. stercorarius*, is represented in the Southeast by two males

collected in Georgia. The larva has been found only in cattle dung (Strenzke 1950; Laurence 1954).

Cardiocladius. Of four described Nearctic species, two occur in the Southeast. Some characteristics of *C. albiplumus* are identical with those of both *Cardiocladius* and *Eukiefferiella*; the generic limits for *Cardiocladius* need to be redefined (Halvorsen and Saether 1987). Some of the apparently undescribed species (known only as larvae) may ultimately prove to be *Eukiefferiella*. The immature stages seem to prefer swiftly flowing waters and some species are fairly tolerant of toxic pollution.

Chaetocladius. The only named species in the Southeast, *C. stamfordi*, occurs in both semiaquatic and aquatic habitats. Various authorities have identified "new species," some of which may prove to be conspecific; we estimate that three are valid. Most species in the genus can probably be best characterized as semiaquatic. A recently described species from Oregon was the first wood-mining member of this genus (Cranston and Oliver 1988b).

Chasmatonotus. The immature stages are not known, except for first instars. Adults in the Southeast are usually collected in wooded areas at higher elevations of the Appalachians.

Clunio. *Clunio* is a worldwide marine genus. In the Southeast, only one species—*marshalli*—has been collected (from the Florida coast).

Compterosmittia. The immature stages for the single southeastern species, *C. nerius*, are unknown. P. S. Cranston (personal communication) stated that the immature stages of a species of *Compterosmittia* known from the Orient are similar to those of *Limnophyes* Eaton and *Paralimnophyes* Brundin and have been collected from fluid in pitcher plants (*Nepenthes* spp.). Cranston and Oliver (1988a) synonymized *C. clavigera* Saether with *Camptocladius nerius*.

Corynoneura. Immature stages and adults are characteristically small and live in a wide variety of aquatic habitats. Larvae are common and widespread in the Southeast, but little taxonomic work has been done on this group; many additional species not listed in Table 3 may occur in the Southeast. *Corynoneura fittkaui*, listed for North Carolina and South Carolina, may eventually prove to represent an undescribed species similar to *C. fittkaui* of Palearctic collections. Species identifications are possible only with males, but preserved larvae can easily be identified to genus by the long antennae.

Cricotopus. Three subgenera are recognized, along with 13 species groups of larvae and 16 species groups of pupae. Nine larval groups occur in North Carolina, plus two unplaced species. The *tibialis, fuscus, laricomalis,* and *brevipalpis* species groups have not been recorded from the Southeast. Several *Cricotopus* species in North Carolina—especially *C. bicinctus* and *C.* near *infuscatus* (Malloch)—are tolerant of pollution. Hirvenoja's (1973) classic monograph of the genus for the western Palearctic (translated by Simpson et al. 1983) is indispensable for identifications, although it does not specifically cover Nearctic species. More recently, LeSage and Harrison (1980) have dealt with 11 species in southern Ontario and Boesel (1983) reviewed the status of 21 species from the Northeast. Species identifications are best made with adult males, although the immature stages of some species are distinctive. The ecology of *C. (Nostococladius) nostocicola* is unique, in that the immature stages live within disks of the alga *Nostoc*. Some larvae and pupae of *C. (Cricotopus)* and *C. (Isocladius)* are difficult to separate from those of *Orthocladius (Orthocladius).*

Diplocladius. The Holarctic species *D. cultriger* is known from the Southeast. However, variation suggests that a cryptic complex of species may be involved. Its larva is found in streams, mainly in winter.

Diplosmittia. Adults matching the description of *D. carinata* are known from Georgia. The immature stages are unknown and are probably terrestrial.

Doithrix. The immature stages for the genus are known from seep areas or margins of small streams and are probably best characterized as semiterrestrial.

Doncricotopus. Species of *Doncricotopus* have been described from the Northwest Territories (Saether 1981a) and Finland (Tuiskunen 1985). The collection of larvae by M. Heyn (personal communication) from Florida and Georgia seems unusual but the records have been verified (D. R. Oliver, personal communication). The genus is similar in all stages to *Rheocricotopus* and *Nanocladius.*

Epoicocladius. The immature stages are found on larval mayflies of the subfamily Ephemerinae. The association appears to be commensalistic. Larvae generally

attach to the gills of their hosts and are found in the bottom of a collecting jar containing this mayfly, presumably after being dislodged and settling to the bottom. A mayfly may harbor up to eight larvae (Tokeshi 1986). The immature stages are distinctive in having many abdominal setae.

Eukiefferiella. Only one species, *E. brevinervis,* has been described to date from the Nearctic. The other species we list (Table 3) are based on adults identified by using European keys. The genus (sensu Thienemann 1926) has been recently revised by Saether and Halvorsen (1981) into a restricted *Eukiefferiella,* an amended *Tvetenia,* and a new genus *Dratnalia,* known only from Europe. The definitive work for Nearctic larvae is that of Bode (1983). No identifications to species of any North American larva of *Eukiefferiella* can as yet be considered valid without an associated adult. Of the 10 larval groups of North American *Eukiefferiella* (Bode 1983), *brehmi, brevicalcar, claripennis, devonica, gracei,* and *pseudomontana* have been collected in the Southeast. The *E. rectangularis* group has been transferred to the genus *Tokunagaia. Eukiefferiella devonica* and *E. ilkleyensis* are reported on the basis of larval and pupal specimens of both, and also adult *E. ilkleyensis.* Halvorsen et al. (1982) pointed out inconsistencies within the *devonica* species group, however, and the records for the species in this group may not hold. Most species of *Eukiefferiella* prefer cool to cold, swift-flowing, oxygenated streams. The genus is most diverse in mountain streams, where it occurs with periphyton or moss. Preserved larvae are often pigmented with blue, green, or red.

Euryhapsis. Only the immatures of one of the four known species are described, all of which occur primarily in western North America. The specimen from North Carolina is an adult, and those from Tennessee are larval specimens near *E. cilium* (W. L. Pennington, personal communication).

Georthocladius. Larvae occur in moist soil and seep areas of small streams and also in hardwood swamps in Florida (D. L. Evans, personal communication). Adults are infrequently collected.

Gymnometriocnemus. Larvae appear to be largely terrestrial, especially in the subgenus *Gymnometriocnemus.*

Heleniella. Immature stages of the two species known in the Southeast, *H. hirta* and *H. parva,* typically occur in low-order streams in winter and early spring. They appear to intergrade as adult males, and may ultimately prove to be a single species.

Heterotrissocladius. Only one species, *H. marcidus*, is known with certainty from the Southeast. At least one undescribed species is known from small coastal plain streams in Georgia and North Carolina, especially in winter. A second undescribed species is common in mountain streams. Most records for northern Nearctic species are from lakes, whereas records from the Southeast are from streams.

Hydrobaenus. An excellent revision of the genus was published by Saether (1976); however, little material was included from the Southeast. It is often difficult to use his key to separate adult males. Larvae appear to be collected most often in winter and early spring.

Krenosmittia. No named species occur in the Southeast. Larvae are usually found in sandy substrates, but are small and difficult to see. Few specimens are collected—which may reflect their small size and hyporheic habitat. Larvae can be recognized by the long anal setae, a character shared with only two other genera, *Parachaetocladius* and *Pseudorthocladius*.

Limnophyes. The immature stages of most species are found in moist soil and decaying vegetation and are not considered aquatic. Cranston and Oliver (1988a) have placed some species in synonymy and modified Saether's (1975b) key to male adults. The genus has been revised by Saether (1990).

Lipurometriocnemus. A male specimen almost identical to the Antillean species *L. glabalus* has been recorded from the coastal plain in Georgia. Apparent differences exist only in the number and placement of acrostichial setae. The immature stages are unknown.

Lopescladius. The relatively small larvae appear to be common in small to large streams in sandy areas over much of the Southeast, but most identifications have been limited to genus. Unmounted larvae can be recognized by their whiplike antennae.

Mesocricotopus. No described species seems to occur in the Southeast, but a pupa near *Mesocricotopus* was collected in Georgia by one of us (B.A.C.). Immature stages have been reported from both lotic and lentic habitats in the Nearctic region.

Mesosmittia. The genus was recently revised by Saether (1985c). Three species, all believed to be terrestrial, occur in the Southeast (mainly Georgia). *Mesosmittia flexuella* (Edwards), which was once thought to have a Holarctic distribution, is now believed to be restricted to the Palearctic.

Metriocnemus. The ecological characteristics of this genus was reviewed by Cranston and Judd (1987), who indicated that immature *Metriocnemus knabi* seem to be restricted to fluids of the pitcher plant. *Metriocnemus fuscipes* has been collected by D. L. Evans (personal communication) from mats of the moss *Polytrichum* sp. in springs in the interior uplands of Tennessee. Saether (1989) reviewed the systematics of the genus and illustrated the immatures of several species.

Nanocladius. The nominate subgenus is widespread, *N. distinctus* being common in many collections from streams. This species, in particular, is tolerant of organic enrichment and is often abundant, with other *Nanocladius* species, in rivers downstream from urban areas. The larva characterized by Mozley (1980) as a genus near *Nanocladius* B is not a *Nanocladius*; its taxonomic position remains unknown. *Nanocladius* (*Plecopteracoluthus*) larvae have been reported to occur symphoretically on immature Perlidae, Corydalidae, and Leptophlebiidae. In Georgia, larval *N.* cf. *branchicolus* have been found only on immature stages of Pteronarcidae in small, mountain streams. Adult males from Georgia are structurally similar to *N. branchicolus*, differing mainly in setal counts.

Oliveridia. The type species of the genus was collected from an Arctic ultraoligotrophic lake, but a second species was later described from a river in Kansas (Ferrington and Saether 1987). Immatures of two species possibly belonging to this genus have been recorded in North Carolina, but one or both may belong to a new genus. Until adult or pupal associations have been made, their exact placement is uncertain.

Orthocladius. Four subgenera are recognized, all represented in the Southeast. Larvae are common and widespread in most streams and rivers, but difficult to identify to species. The Nearctic species of the subgenus *Orthocladius* were revised by Soponis (1977), who provided excellent keys to all stages; however, several undescribed species still remain in the Southeast.

The occurrence of setal tufts has been a traditional character for distinguishing larvae of some species of

Cricotopus from larvae of all species of *Orthocladius*; however, the larva of *Orthocladius* (*O.*) *annectens* has *Cricotopus*-like setal tufts on the abdomen (Fagnani and Soponis 1988). The presence of setal tufts on the abdomen of *Symposiocladius lignicola* led Cranston and Oliver (1988b) to transfer the genus *Symposiocladius* (Cranston 1982b) to a subgenus of *Orthocladius*. This is the same species as "genus undetermined" *acutilabis* Konstantinov, which had been tentatively placed in the genus *Cricotopus* in recent years.

Orthocladius (*Symposiocladius*) larvae are wood miners in flowing waters. The species appears to be an obligate xylophage, creating tunnels or passages in soft, decomposing hardwoods. Cranston and Oliver (1988b) presented new systematic and ecological information for this and several other xylophytic chironomids.

Parachaetocladius. *Parachaetocladius abnobaeus* is usually found in mountain streams. The larvae are most often associated with substrates of mixed gravel and sand and are sometimes difficult to locate. Studies in Kansas by Ferrington (1987) and Barton et al. (1987) in Ontario suggested a hyporheic habitat for *P. abnobaeus*. A similar habitat in the Southeast is evident from pupal exuviae, which are abundant in drift samples in areas where larvae are scarce. Cranston and Oliver (1988a) synonymized *P. hudsoni* with *P. abnobaeus*.

Paracricotopus. Larvae are often found in hygropetric habitats in the Southeast. Species identifications are probably best made with pupae. Some species of this genus can be easily confused with some species of *Eukiefferiella*. All known southeastern species have been illustrated (Saether 1980a; Steiner 1983; Caldwell 1985). Only *P. millrockensis* is more commonly found in streams.

Parakiefferiella. The genus is poorly known but occurs commonly in both lotic and lentic waters in the Southeast. On the basis of both larval and adult specimens, at least five or six undescribed species occur in this region. Larvae are fairly common in the littoral regions of reservoirs and in small sandy piedmont and sandhill streams. This genus may be poorly collected due to the small size and interstitial (psammophilic) habitat of some species. The superficial similarity of immatures and adults of *Parakiefferiella* to those of *Rheosmittia* has resulted in some confusion—for example, the records of Benke et al. (1979) for *Parakiefferiella* in the Satilla River, Georgia, represent *Rheosmittia*. *Rheosmittia* was originally placed as a subgenus of *Parakiefferiella* by Brundin (1956).

Parametriocnemus. Larvae are relatively common in all the southeastern States. The occurrence of several undescribed species limits our comments on distribution. Larvae of *P. lundbecki* preserved in ethanol are sometimes slightly purplish, and faint stripes extend from the eyespots. Larvae of this species may be the most common chironomid found in clean streams of the piedmont and mountains.

Paraphaenocladius. The genus is generally considered to be terrestrial to semiaquatic. Some larvae may not be easily separable from *Parametriocnemus*, and the curved preanal segment may become distorted in mounting. B. Bilyj (personal communication) suggested using the relative length of the second antennal segment to the remaining segments ($A_2 \leqslant A_{3-5}$) and the shape of the ventromental plate to separate the genera (see Cranston et al. 1983).

Paratrichocladius. The larvae are difficult to separate from some *Cricotopus* (s.s.) and *Orthocladius*—hence the limited recognition in the region. Rossaro (1979) described the larva of *P. rufiventris*. The two undescribed species are based on adults from the coastal plains and mountains of South Carolina. Identifications based solely on larvae are highly suspect.

Platysmittia. The immature stages are unknown. Adult males of the one species described from the Southeast, *P. fimbriata*, were collected near a spring, whereas adults of the other known species, *P. bilyji*, were caught in an emergence trap set on a small stream in Manitoba (B. Bilyj, personal communication).

Plhudsonia. The larval stage is unknown; pupae were recovered from a spring, a seep area of the spring, and the stream fed by the spring. Male genitalia superficially resemble those of *Diplocladius* and other genera having a bifid gonostylus.

Psectrocladius. All four subgenera are known from the Southeast. *Psectrocladius* often inhabits acidic habitats in the Southeast. Identifications to subgenera and species are often futile, even with reared specimens. Failure to recognize the presence of a larval cardinal beard can cause confusion with *Nanocladius*, some of which have a similar mentum. However, in alcohol they can easily be separated by size alone (*Nanocladius* is about one-third to one-fourth the size of *Psectrocladius*); additionally, the eye spots are configured differently (B. Bilyj, personal communication).

Pseudorthocladius. Specimens are generally collected near small streams, in seeps, and in the floodplains of rivers. The genus was revised by Saether and Sublette (1983).

Pseudosmittia. Larvae are occasionally found in streams, but the typical habitat appears to be terrestrial to semiaquatic. One undescribed species is common in the wet bank area of the Savannah River below Hartwell Dam. High water release flow for peak power production wets this habitat almost daily. Adults are most common in the piedmont region of Georgia in late summer and early fall. Cranston and Oliver (1988a) reported *P. digitata* from Florida. Similar adult males occur in Georgia. A revision of the genus is in preparation (L. C. Ferrington, personal communication).

Psilometriocnemus. The immature stages are known from seeps, damp soil, and springs. Larvae are similar to (and thus can be confused with) those of *Parametriocnemus* and *Paraphaenocladius.* Cranston and Oliver (1988a) have synonymized *Psilometriocnemus cristatus* with *P. triannulatus.*

Rheocricotopus. Saether (1985d), who revised the species for the Holarctic region, gave generic diagnoses for all stages, and recognized two subgenera. *Rheocricotopus robacki* is one of the most widely distributed lotic species in the Southeast.

Rheosmittia. Immature stages are psammophilic, very small, and when preserved in ethanol usually have a purplish body pigmentation. The genus is sometimes very abundant in the coarse-sand substrate of larger streams and rivers. However, the forms are often undercollected because they are small and sand substrates are often not adequately sampled. The genitalia of both sexes of *Rheosmittia* are nearly identical to those of many species of *Parakiefferiella.* No species of *Rheosmittia* have yet been described from North America, even though undescribed species (two or more) are widespread in all regions of the Southeast.

Saetheriella. This genus is monotypic and known only from the adult male. The immature stages are probably terrestrial or semiaquatic, as judged by the general area where adults have been collected.

Smittia. Species of the genus are generally terrestrial and can commonly be found in the soils of greenhouses

(Webb 1982). Species identifications are usually impossible. Webb (1982) has described the immatures of *S. lasiops.* Revision of the genus is needed.

Stilocladius. The one species, *S. clinopecten,* is known from the Southeast. It is small, most commonly found during cold weather and in small streams. It keys to Genus near *Nanocladius* A of Mozley (1980).

Sublettiella. This monotypic genus is known only from the male.

Symbiocladius. Species of this unique genus are probably obligate parasites on mayfly nymphs. In Georgia, *S. chattahoocheensis* has been found on the heptageniid mayfly larva *Epeorus,* near *vitreus.*

Synorthocladius. Larvae live in rivers and streams and have also been found in a riverine area of a reservoir. At least two species appear to occur in the Southeast, as judged from larval and adult specimens. The larvae have a unique mentum and long radiating beard. Unmounted larvae often contain a blue-green pigment that is commonly retained in the adult.

Thienemannia. One species, *T. pilinucha,* is known from the eastern area of Tennessee from a male only. The larval stage of a Palearctic species is found in springs and hygropetric habitats.

Thienemanniella. Species are relatively small and the genus is widespread. There are no keys for species identifications of the immature stages; the genus needs to be revised.

Tokunagaia. The genus was revised by Halvorsen and Saether (1987), who included the *Eukiefferiella rectangularis* group in the genus *Tokunagaia.* An undetermined species has recently been found on a wet granitic outcrop in mountainous western North Carolina by one of us (B.A.C.)—a habitat not previously reported for the genus.

Tvetenia. Species of this genus were formerly part of *Eukiefferiella.* Immature stages are generally separable to species group only, but the larvae are common and widespread. The work of Bode (1983) is useful for larval identifications to species groups. The larva of *T. vitracies* of the *discoloripes* group was described by Mason (1985a).

Unniella. This is an abundant winter species commonly collected in coastal plain streams. The larva keys to Genus near *Oliveridia* in Mozley (1980).

Xylotopus. One of the two known species occurs throughout the Southeast. The large larvae mine decaying, waterlogged hardwood in slower reaches of streams and shallow standing water. The genus was reviewed by Oliver (1985). Unmounted larvae can be recognized by the dark head, white body, and an abdominal hair fringe.

Zalutschia. Specimens of *Zalutschia* are most commonly collected in lakes, although some species live in streams. Two species are described from the Southeast and at least two apparently undescribed species occur in coastal plain streams. Most species in the genus are northern forms.

Genus near *Georthocladius.* The taxon is represented by a small pupa collected at a seep in Great Smoky Mountains National Park. The pupa also has affinities toward *Parasmittia* and we assume that it occupies a semiaquatic to terrestrial habitat. The larval and adult stages are unknown.

Orthocladiinae sp. A. The taxon is represented by a pupa of a species belonging to the *Brillia* group with closest affinities to *Euryhapsis* (Saether 1982). The larval and adult stages are unknown.

Orthocladiinae sp. B. The taxon is represented by a pupa of a species showing relationship with *Psilometriocnemus* and the *Cardiocladius* group. The larval and adult stages are unknown.

Orthocladiinae sp. C. The larvae are similar to those of species in the genus *Acamptocladius.* This larval type possibly represents *Platysmittia fimbriata* (Saether 1982). The same larva was reported as "Genus near *Rheosmittia*" by Mozley (1980).

Chironominae

The greatest number of chironomid species in the Southeast are in the subfamily Chironominae. We have recorded 66 genera and 323 species, of which 8 genera and at least 118 species are undescribed (Table 4). An immature stage has been illustrated for six of the eight undescribed genera, but for only nine of the undescribed species. *Polypedilum* has the greatest number of species at 47; *Tanytarsus* ranks second with 30 and *Cryptochironomus* third with 17. Most of the genera have only one to three species.

Of the species of Chironominae with known habitats, 128 occur in lakes, 99 in streams, and 86 in rivers. One marine species is known but no species have been described from terrestrial habitats. We have collected undescribed species of *Paratendipes* and *Tanytarsus* from terrestrial habitats. Most of the Chironominae have been collected in Florida (151), South Carolina (150), and North Carolina (134). A clear majority is from the coastal plain (170), followed by the piedmont (138) and the mountains (46).

Apedilum. Until Epler (1988a) reviewed the genus, its species had been placed in *Paralauterborniella.* Both species in the genus occur in the Southeast.

Asheum. This genus name replaces *Pedionomus.* Despite the similarity of its larvae to *Polypedilum*, *Asheum* is a valid genus, with one known species, *A. beckae* (see Pinder and Reiss 1986). It is common in coastal lakes and canals, large rivers, and the Florida Everglades.

Axarus. The genus *Axarus* of Pinder and Reiss (1983) replaces the *Xenochironomus* (*Anceus*) of Roback (1963). Most North Carolina larvae belong to a group of species with flat and light mandibular teeth.

Beckidia. The single record for *Beckidia*, which replaces *Beckiella*, is based on an undescribed adult from the Savannah River Plant in South Carolina. The larva has been reported only from sandy deposits of large rivers.

Chernovskiia. This genus occurs interstitially in the coarse sand of lakes and (especially) large rivers. Larvae were illustrated by Saether (1977b).

Chironomus. Larval illustrations have been published for *C. crassicaudatus* and *C. staegeri* by Wülker et al. (1971) and for *C. stigmaterus* by Sublette and Sublette (1974). Webb and Scholl (1985) published morphological characters that are useful in identifying larvae of the European species of *Chironomus. Chaetolabis*, treated here as a subgenus, was raised to generic status by Yamamoto (1987), but we consider this change questionable and here follow Webb et al. (1987).

Chironomus is often associated with conditions of low dissolved oxygen. However, only *C. riparius* and *C. decorus* are consistently associated with polluted conditions;

Table 4. *Summary of distribution and habitat for Chironominae in the southeastern United States. Habitat: L = lakes (natural, impoundments, swamps), M = marine, R = river (>12 m wide), S = streams (≤12 m wide), Sp = seeps or springs, T = terrestrial. Regions (see Figure for locations): C = Coastal Plain including Sandhills, I = Interior Upland, M = Mountains (Ridge and Valley and Appalachian), P = Piedmont Plateau.*

Genus, subgenus, species, and author	AL	FL	GA	NC	SC	TN	Habitat	Region	Reference[b]
Apedilum									8
elachistus Townes	x	x	x				L	C	
subcinctum Townes		x		x			L	CP	
Asheum									30
beckae (Sublette)	x	x	x	x	x		R,L	CP	
Axarus									22
dorneri Malloch		x						C	
festivus (Say)	x	x	x		x	x	LR	I	
rogersi (Beck and Beck)		x	x	x	x		LRS	CP	
taenionotus (Say)		x	x		x		LS	CP	
Beckidia		x			x		S	C	27
Chernovskiia									27
orbicus (Townes)		x		x	x		LR	CP	
Chironomus									34
(Chaetolabis)									
ochreatus (Townes)		x	x		x		L	CP	
(Chironomus)									
crassicaudatus Malloch	x	x	x	x	x	x	L	C	
decorus (Johannsen)	x	x	x	x	x	x	LRS	CIMP	
plumosus (Linnaeus)	x	x		x			LR	CP	
pungens (Townes)		x		x			L	CP	
riparius Meigen		x		x	x		LRS	CP	
staegeri Lundbeck	x	x		x	x	x	L	C	
stigmaterus (Say)		x	x				L	C	
tuxis Curran		x			x		L	C	
undescribed species (5+)									
Cladopelma									1
amachaerus (Townes)	x	x			x		LR	CP	
boydi (Beck)	x	x	x		x	x	RS	CIP	
collator (Townes)		x	x	x	x		L	CP	
edwardsi (Kruseman)		x	x	x	x		L	P	
galeator (Townes)		x	x		x		L	C	
viridulus (Linnaeus)		x			x	x	RS	C	
undescribed species (2+)									
Cladotanytarsus									15
viridiventris Malloch	x			x	x			P	
undescribed species (9+)									
Constempellina									15
brevicosta (Edwards)	x			x	x		S	M	
undescribed species (2+)									
Cryptochironomus									6, 12
argus Roback			x					P	
blarina Townes		x		x	x		L	CP	
digitatus (Malloch)		x						C	
fulvus (Johannsen)	x	x		x	x		LR	CMP	

Table 4. *Continued.*

Genus, subgenus, species, and author	AL	FL	GA	NC	SC	TN	Habitat	Region	Reference[b]
				State[a]					
parafulvus (Beck and Beck)		x	x				S	C	
ponderosus (Sublette)		x		x	x		L	CMP	
scimitarus Townes		x		x	x		L	CP	
sorex Townes		x		x	x		L	CP	
styliferus (Johannsen)		x						C	
undescribed species (8+)									
"*Cryptochironomus*" Pagast (1933)				x			R	C	27
"*Cryptochironomus*"									27
nr. *macropodus* Lyakhov			x	x			R	C	
Cryptotendipes									27
casuarius (Townes)		x						C	
emorsus (Townes)		x		x	x		L	CP	
pseudotener (Goetgh.)					x			C	
Demeijerea									15
atrimanus (Coquillett)	x	x			x		LS	P	
brachialis (Coquillett)	x			x				CP	
obreptus (Townes)				x	x			M	
Demicryptochironomus									27
cuneatus (Townes)	x		x	x	x		LS	CP	
undescribed species (2+)									
Dicrotendipes									7
botaurus (Townes)						x	LRS	CMP	
fumidus (Johannsen)	x	x	x	x	x	x	LRS	P	
leucoscelis (Townes)		x			x		L	C	
lobus (E. C. Beck)		x	x	x	x		LR		
lucifer (Johannsen)	x	x	x	x	x	x	LR	MP	
modestus (Say)	x	x	x	x	x	x	LRS	CP	
neomodestus (Malloch)	x	x	x	x	x	x	LRS	CP	
nervosus (Staeger)	x	x		x	x	x	L	CP	
simpsoni Epler	x	x	x	x	x	x	LRS	CP	
thanatogratus Epler		x			x		S	C	
tritomus Kieffer		x	x	x	x		L	CP	
undescribed species (1+)									
Einfeldia									15
austini Beck and Beck		x					S	C	
brunneipennis (Johannsen)	x	x		x				C	
chelonia (Townes)				x	x			P	
dorsalis (Meigen)		x	x	x	x			CP	
natchitocheae Sublette		x	x	x	x	x	LS	CMP	
pagana (Meigen)				x			L	P	
Endochironomus									9
nigricans (Johannsen)	x	x	x	x	x	x	LR	CP	
subtendens (Townes)		x			x		LR	CM	
undescribed species (1)									
Endotribelos									9
hesperium (Sublette)		x			x		LRS	C	
Gillotia									27
alboviridis (Malloch)					x		S	P	

Table 4. *Continued.*

Genus, subgenus, species, and author	AL	FL	GA	NC	SC	TN	Habitat	Region	Reference[b]
Glyptotendipes									15
(Glyptotendipes)									
seminole Townes		x						C	
(Phytotendipes)									
ampius Townes						x	L	I	
barbipes (Staeger)			x	x			L	CP	
dreisbachi Townes				x			L	P	
lobiferus (Say)		x	x	x	x		L	CP	
meridionalis Sublette	x	x	x	x	x	x	L	CP	
paripes (Edwards)	x	x	x	x	x		L	CP	
testaceus Townes		x	x	x	x		LS	CP	
undescribed species (3)									
Goeldichironomus									17
amazonicus (Fittkau)		x					L	C	
carus (Townes)		x	x				LR	C	
devineyae (Beck)		x	x				L	C	
fluctuans Reiss		x						C	
holoprasinus (Goeldi)	x	x	x	x	x	x	LRS	CP	
natans Reiss		x						C	
pictus Reiss		x						C	
Harnischia									26
curtilamellata (Malloch)	x	x	x	x	x	x	LR	CP	
undescribed species (1)									
Hyporhygma									18
quadripunctatum (Malloch)		x	x	x			LR	C	
Kiefferulus									2
(Kiefferulus)									
dux (Johannsen)		x	x	x	x		LRS	CP	
(Wirthiella)				x			L	P	
Kloosia									19
dorsenna Saether			x	x			S	CP	
Lauterborniella									15
agrayloides (Kieffer)		x		x	x	x	LR	CM	
Lipiniella			x	x	x	x	LRS	IMP	15
Microchironomus									11
nigrovittatus (Malloch)	x	x	x	x		x	LRS	CMP	
undescribed species (1)									
Micropsectra									25
undescribed species (6+)			x	x	x		LRS	CMP	
Microtendipes									14
anticus (Walker)			x					C	
caducus Townes	x		x	x			RS	MP	
caelum Townes					x		S	CP	
pedellus (DeGeer)	x	x	x	x	x	x	LRS	CMP	
undescribed species (2+)									
Genus nr. *Microtendipes* A			x		x		R	C	21
Genus nr. *Microtendipes* B		x					L	C	See text

Table 4. *Continued.*

Genus, subgenus, species, and author	AL	FL	GA	NC	SC	TN	Habitat	Region	Reference[b]
Nilothauma									15
bicornis (Townes)		x	x	x	x		L	CP	
babiyi (Rempel)		x			x		L	CP	
mirabilis (Townes)		x			x			C	
undescribed species (1+)									
Nimbocera									31
pinderi (Steiner and Hurlbert)		x	x	x	x		LRS	C	
Genus nr. *Nimbocera*		x	x		x		L	C	32
Omisus									28, 2
pica Townes		x		x	x		LR	C	
undescribed species (1+)									
Pagastiella									33
ostansa (Webb)	x	x	x	x	x	x	LRS	CP	
undescribed species (1)									
Parachironomus									1
abortivus (Malloch)				x	x		L	CP	
alatus (Beck)		x					LS	C	
carinatus (Townes)	x	x	x	x	x	x	LRS	CP	
chaetoala (Sublette)				x				P	
directus (Dendy and Sublette)	x	x	x				LRS	CP	
frequens (Johannsen)	x	x	x	x	x	x	R	CP	
hirtalatus (Beck and Beck)		x					LS	C	
monochromus (Wulp)	x	x	x	x	x		LRS	CMP	
pectinatellae (Dendy and Sublette)	x	x	x	x	x		LR	P	
potamogeti (Townes)		x		x	x		L	CP	
schneideri (Beck and Beck)		x	x	x			LR	CP	
sublettei (Beck)		x	x				LRS	C	
tenuicaudatus (Malloch)	x	x		x		x	LR	CP	
undescribed species (1+)									
Paracladopelma									10
doris (Townes)		x		x	x		RS	C	
loganae (Beck and Beck)	x	x	x	x	x		RS	C	
nereis (Townes)	x	x	x	x	x		LRS	MP	
undine (Townes)		x	x	x	x		LRS	CMP	
sp. 1 sensu Jackson				x			S	CP	
sp. 2 sensu Jackson			x	x			S	MP	
Paralauterborniella									15
nigrohalteralis (Malloch)		x	x	x	x		LRS	CMP	
undescribed species (1)									
Parapsectra Reiss				x			S	M	15
Paratanytarsus									20
dissimilis Johannsen					x		S	P	
dubius (Malloch)	x							P	
recens (Sublette)				x	x		LS	CP	
undescribed species (2+)									
Paratendipes									15
albimanus (Meigen)	x		x	x	x	x	LS	P	
basidens (Townes)	x							C	

Table 4. Continued.

Genus, subgenus, species, and author	AL	FL	GA	NC	SC	TN	Habitat	Region	Reference[b]
	State[a]								
nitidulus (Coquillett)					x		R	P	
subaequalis (Malloch)		x	x				RS	C	
"connectens" gr.		x	x	x			R	CP	35
undescribed species (1)									9
Phaenopsectra								C	
dyari (Townes)		x						C	
flavipes (Meigen)	x	x	x	x	x	x	RS	P	
obediens (Johannsen)	x	x	x	x	x	x	RS	P	
punctipes (Wiedemann)					x			P	
vittata (Townes)		x			x		L	CMP	
undescribed species (2)									3
Polypedilum									
(Pentapedilum)									
albulum Townes		x						C	
sordens (van der Wulp)					x			C	
tritum (Walker)		x	x	x	x		LRS	CM	
undescribed species (7)									
(Polypedilum)									
albicorne (Meigen)		x			x		S	CP	
angustum Townes		x					LS	C	
aviceps Townes	x	x	x	x	x	x	S	CMP	
braseniae (Leathers)		x	x	x	x		L	CP	
cinctum Townes				x	x		R	P	
convictum (Walker)	x	x	x	x	x	x	RS	CMP	
fallax (Johannsen)	x	x	x	x	x	x	LRS	CMP	
illinoense (Malloch)	x	x	x	x	x	x	LRS	CMP	
laetum (Meigen)	x	x	x	x	x		S	CP	
nigritum Townes		x						C	
ontario (Walley)			x				RS	C	
pedatum Townes					x		Sp	CP	
sordens (van der Wulp)		x			x			C	
sulaceps Townes					x			C	
trigonus Townes		x	x					P	
vibex Townes		x						C	
walleyi Townes					x		S	M	
undescribed species (5+)									
(Tripodura)									
albinodus Townes					x		L	P	
digitifer Townes	x	x		x	x	x	L	MP	
floridense Townes		x					L	C	
gomphus Townes		x			x		RS	CP	
griseopunctatum Malloch		x		x	x		R	CP	
halterale (Coquillett)	x	x	x	x	x	x	LRS	CMP	
obtusum Townes		x			x			CP	
parascalaenum Beck		x	x	x	x		LRS	CP	
pardus Townes					x		S	C	
parvum Townes	x	x						C	
pterospilus Townes		x						C	
scalaenum (Schrank)	x	x	x	x	x		LRS	CMP	

Table 4. *Continued.*

Genus, subgenus, species, and author	AL	FL	GA	NC	SC	TN	Habitat	Region	Reference[b]
			State[a]						
simulans Townes	x	x		x	x		L	CP	
undescribed species (2)									
Pontomyia Edwards		x					M	C	5
Pseudochironomus									27
fulviventris (Johannsen)		x		x	x		L	CP	
julia (Curran)		x		x	x		LRS	CP	
middlekauffi Townes		x					L	C	
rex Hauber		x	x	x			L	CP	
richardsoni Malloch	x	x		x			LRS	CP	
undescribed species (1+)									
Rheotanytarsus									16
pellucidas Walker					x		S	C	
undescribed species (5+)									
Robackia									27
claviger (Townes)	x	x	x	x	x		RS	CMP	
demeijerei (Kruseman)	x	x	x	x	x	x	RS	CMP	
undescribed species (1)									
Saetheria									29
hirta Saether				x	x		S	P	
tylus (Townes)	x		x	x	x		LRS	CMP	
undescribed species (1)									
Stelechomyia									18
perpulchra (Mitchell)		x	x	x	x		RS	CP	
Stempellina									32
almi Brundin			x	x	x		S	C	
bausei (Kieffer)					x		S	MP	
rodesta Webb					x		L	P	
subglabripennis (Brundin)				x			L	P	
undescribed species (4+)									
Stempellinella									15
brevis (Edwards)					x		S	C	
leptocelloides (Webb)					x		S	C	
undescribed species (1+)									
Stenochironomus									
(*Petalopholeus*)									4
aestivalis Townes		x	x	x	x		LRS	CP	
browni Townes		x						C	
cinctus Townes		x	x	x	x		L	CMP	
(*Stenochironomus*)									
hilaris (Walker)	x	x	x	x	x	x	LRS	CIMP	
macateei (Malloch)	x	x	x	x	x		LRS	CMP	
poecilopterus (Mitchell)		x	x	x	x		LRS	CMP	
unictus Townes	x	x	x	x	x		LRS	CMP	
undescribed species (1)									
Stictochironomus									13
annulicrus Townes				x		x	Sp	M	
devinctus (Say)		x	x	x	x		LRS	CP	
palliatus (Coquillett)	x	x		x			L	CP	

Table 4. *Continued.*

Genus, subgenus, species, and author	AL	FL	GA	NC	SC	TN	Habitat	Region	Reference[b]
Sublettea									24
coffmani (Roback)	x		x	x	x		RS	MP	
Tanytarsus									32
buckleyi Sublette					x		S	C	
confusus Malloch	x	x		x	x		LS	CP	
debilis (Meigen)				x			L	M	
dendyi Sublette	x			x	x		LS	CP	
guerlus Roback					x		S	C	
holochlorus (Edwards)				x	x		L	P	
neoflavellus (Malloch)	x			x	x		L	MP	
recurvatus Brundin				x	x		LS	CP	
tibialis Webb					x		S	C	
xanthus Sublette	x							P	
undescribed species (20+)									
Tribelos									9
atrum (Townes)		x	x	x			L	CP	
fuscicorne (Malloch)	x	x	x	x	x	x	LRS	CP	
jucundum (Walker)	x	x	x	x	x		RS	CMP	
undescribed species (2)									
Xenochironomus									22
xenolabis (Kieffer)	x	x	x	x	x	x	LRS	CMP	
undescribed species (1)									
Xestochironomus									4
subletti Borkent		x	x	x	x		LRS	CP	
Zavrelia									15
undescribed species (3+)				x	x				
Zavreliella									15
varipennis (Coquillett)		x	x	x	x		LRS	CP	
Chironomini Genus A		x			x		LR	P	23
Chironomini Genus B	x			x	x		L	P	15
Chironomini Genus C		x					S	C	See text

[a] States: AL, Alabama; FL, Florida; GA, Georgia; NC, North Carolina; SC, South Carolina; TN, Tennessee.

[b] References: (1) Beck and Beck 1969b; (2) Beck and Beck 1970; (3) Boesel 1985; (4) Borkent 1984; (5) Bretschko 1981; (6) Curry 1958; (7) Epler 1987; (8) Epler 1988a; (9) Grodhaus 1987; (10) Jackson 1977; (11) Kugler 1971; (12) Mason 1985b; (13) Mason 1985c; (14) Pinder 1976; (15) Pinder and Reiss 1983; (16) Pinder and Reiss 1986; (17) Reiss 1974; (18) Reiss 1982; (19) Reiss 1988; (20) Reiss and Säwedal 1981; (21) Roback 1953; (22) Roback 1963; (23) Roback 1966; (24) Roback 1975; (25) Säwedal 1982; (26) Saether 1971; (27) Saether 1977b; (28) Saether 1980b; (29) Saether 1983b; (30) Sublette 1964; (31) Steiner and Hulbert 1982; (32) Steiner et al. 1982; (33) Webb 1969; (34) Webb and Scholl 1985; (35) Chernovskii 1949.

of these, only *C. riparius* is consistently found in lotic habitats. Both *C. crassicaudatus* and *C. decorus* were listed as nuisance species by Beck and Beck (1969a) because of mass emergences of adults. Although most species of *Chironomus* feed on detritus, Loden (1974) indicated that *C. decorus* is a facultative predator of oligochaetes. Most *Chironomus* larvae burrow in soft sediments but R. P. Rutter (personal communication) found larvae of the *C. plumosus* group in burrows made by the lepidopteran *Bellura* in the stems of *Nuphar*. Some *Chironomus* larvae in the Tennessee River system reach a length of 55 mm.

Cladopelma. This genus is most often found in lakes, although it may occur in slow-moving portions of streams and rivers. Many species were illustrated (as

Harnischia) by Beck and Beck (1969b). A number of larvae recorded in the Southeast do not fit the described species. Good separation characters are head capsule coloration, position of ventromental plate striations, antennal characteristics, and the shape of the outermost teeth of the mentum.

Cladotanytarsus. The only described species known to occur in the Southeast is *C. viridiventris*, but unpublished work by one of us (D. S.) indicated that at least nine larval types exist. The habitats of these undescribed species seem to be equally divided between lotic and lentic. Most forms are widely distributed from the coast to the mountains, but one species is found primarily in acidic coastal plain streams and one has been collected only in Florida. Most *Cladotanytarsus* larvae live in sand substrates and consequently many show considerable wear on the mentum.

Bilyj and Davies (1989), who described the adults and pupae of seven new species of *Cladotanytarsus* from Manitoba, found the pupae to have better diagnostic characters than the male adults and provided a pupal key to distinguish 20 of 21 Holarctic species.

Constempellina. This genus is limited to small, cool mountain streams. It has a portable, heavy sand case, and may be poorly collected by the usual disturbance-type samplers (Surber, screen). Collection of adults near a mountain stream in South Carolina suggested that three species of *Constempellina* were present—*C. brevicosta* and two undescribed species (T. J. Wilda, personal communication). Larvae of *Constempellina* have also been collected from mountain streams in Alabama (Steiner et al. 1982) and in North Carolina. Characters of the frontoclypeal setae indicated that these were different species.

Cryptochironomus. Work on the pupae of this genus indicated that a large number of undescribed species may exist; however, the separation of larvae and adults may be more difficult. Work on pupae from Lake Norman, North Carolina (Wingo 1983), indicated that six new species might be present. Many of the listed species, especially *C. fulvus*, should be regarded as a complex of closely related species (Mason 1985b). *Cryptochironomus* appears to be a facultative predator of oligochaetes and smaller midges (Darby 1962).

"*Cryptochironomus*" sensu Pagast and "*C.*" near *macropodus* sensu Lyakhov. A larva, similar to that described by Pagast (1933) from Europe, was collected from the Black River, North Carolina, and a specimen similar to that described by Lyakhov (1941) from Russia was collected in the Lumber River, North Carolina. These species may be identified by using the keys of Saether (1977b).

Cryptotendipes. Larval collections of the North Carolina Department of Environmental Management include three species. Most of the described species have been taken from lakes, but an unassociated larva is commonly collected from "enriched" sandy streams in all physiographic regions.

Demeijerea. Larvae of this genus mine in sponges and bryozoans. Specimens are collected infrequently, but this infrequency may partly reflect the paucity of investigation into this unusual habitat. The adults are closely related to *Glyptotendipes*—and *D. obreptus* may indeed be a *Glyptotendipes*. Knowledge of the immatures, currently undescribed, would help to confirm or disprove this identification (M. Heyn, personal communication). *Demeijerea* was formerly a subgenus of *Glyptotendipes*.

Demicryptochironomus. Larvae of this genus are characteristic of clean sandy areas of streams and rivers of the Southeast. Only the larva of *D. cuneatus* has been described (Saether 1977b); it is probably the only species in the Southeast that occurs in lakes. Most larval specimens from streams and rivers differ from *D. cuneatus* in having sharper, more-pointed teeth on the mandible. At least two unassociated species are present—one in the mountains and one in the coastal plain. It is likely that the mountain species is *D. fastigata* (Townes), the other species of *Demicryptochironomus* known from the Nearctic region.

Dicrotendipes. Pinder and Reiss (1983) indicated that *Dicrotendipes* rarely occurs in streams and rivers, but we found this genus to be common in any type of "enriched" habitat, including flowing water. *Dicrotendipes fumidus* was an abundant member of the macrobenthos of the Savannah River where flows reached 1.8 m sec^{-1} (Hudson and Nichols 1986). The Nearctic *Dicrotendipes* were revised by Epler (1987) and the revision was updated by Epler (1988b), but one or more undescribed species remain in the Southeast. Epler (1988b) synonymized *D. incurvus* (Sublette) with *D. tritomus*. Records published before 1987—especially records of *D. nervosus*—should be viewed with caution. Larvae of three common species were illustrated by Simpson and Bode (1980); their data indicated that these taxa—especially *D. neomodestus*—were tolerant of nutrient addition and organic wastes. Some species in the *nervosus* group (including *D. simpsoni*) are also tolerant of toxic wastes. Other species may have a more limited distribution (e.g., *D. lobus* is restricted to coastal marshes and estuaries).

Einfeldia. Members of the genus *Einfeldia* occur most frequently in lentic habitats (often in slightly enriched areas), but the larvae are also found in lotic situations in the Southeast. Most larvae have not been associated with adults, but Beck and Beck (1970) illustrated the larva of *E. austini*, and Sublette (1964) the larva of *E. natchitocheae*.

Endochironomus. The littoral area of mesotrophic lakes is the frequent habitat of *Endochironomus nigricans*. The larvae overwinter in cocoons. This species has also been reared from the bryozoan *Plumatella* (Dendy and Sublette 1959). Simpson and Bode (1980) suggested that this species is typical of high nutrient and organic levels in medium to large rivers. *Endochironomus subtendens* seems to be rare in the Southeast, and also has been associated with eutrophic conditions. Both species were illustrated by Simpson and Bode (1980). The genus has been revised by Grodhaus (1987).

Endotribelos. Sublette (1960) originally described *E. hesperium* in the genus *Tribelos*. Grodhaus (1987) erected a new genus based on all stages. This species has been collected in Florida, where it was associated with aquatic macrophytes.

Gillotia. Identification of this genus was based on the exuvia of a single pupa. Records have previously been limited to the Midwest.

Glyptotendipes. The genus *Glyptotendipes* frequently occurs in eutrophic waters, in ponds, lakes, and slow-moving rivers. Most of the records are attributed to occurrences of *G. barbipes*, *G. lobiferus*, and *G. paripes*. Beck and Beck (1969a) indicated that both *G. lobiferus* and *G. paripes* are considered nuisance species in Florida during mass emergences of adults. One form, *G. barbipes*, is often abundant in sewage oxidation ponds and is somewhat tolerant of brackish water. It was extensively illustrated by Sublette and Sublette (1973). Simpson and Bode (1980) indicated that *G. lobiferus* was very tolerant of sewage wastes in slow-moving rivers and streams of New York; they stated that larvae of this species "build large tubular cases which are permanently attached to the substrate." This species (and probably other closely related ones) is a filter-feeder (Walshe 1951).

Goeldichironomus. The status of *Goeldichironomus* in the Southeast was recently reviewed by J. S. Doughman (personal communication), who relied heavily on the work of Reiss (1974). Most of the species are tropical; known distributions are limited to Georgia and Florida. All species are adapted to mineralized, productive standing waters with fluctuating levels and floating vegetation. *Goeldichironomus holoprasinus* is well adapted to life in temporary pools and is widely distributed. It occurs in some unusual habitats, including tree holes, bird baths, and wading pools, and may also be found in polluted conditions, including sewage lagoons and enriched ponds or streams. *Goeldichironomus devineyae* has been collected in brackish water environments. Beck and Beck (1969a) indicated that both *G. holoprasinus* and *G. carus* may be nuisance species in Florida because of mass emergences of adults in summer.

Harnischia. All stages of *H. curtilamellata* were described by Saether (1971). This species is common in lentic habitats throughout the Southeast, although it is rarely abundant. A larva of a second, undescribed species was collected by one of us (D. S.) from the Cumberland River in Tennessee. The mentum on this specimen appeared to have a notched, light median tooth and three dark lateral teeth, although the outermost lateral tooth was probably composed of three or four fused teeth. This was possibly the undescribed larva of *H. incidata* (Townes).

Hyporhygma. Larvae of *H. quadripunctatum* have been reported to mine in the stems and leaves of *Nymphaea* (Pinder and Reiss 1983). Carpenter (1928) reported the species mining in *Nymphaea* (now *Nuphar*) *advena*. In Georgia, the species has been found mining stems of *Nymphaea odorata*. There are distribution records for Florida, Georgia, and North Carolina, but the collection sites listed by Townes (1945) suggested that it should occur along the entire East Coast.

Kiefferulus. The larva of *K. dux* was described by Beck and Beck (1970). It was found in many small lotic and lentic water bodies, including streams polluted by organic wastes. The subgenus *Wirthiella* has been collected in a South Carolina reservoir (M. Heyn, personal communication).

Kloosia. This genus was previously recognized as *Oschia* by Saether (1983b), from adults collected near the Savannah River Plant, South Carolina. Perhaps some unusual larvae that have occasionally been collected from sand substrates of piedmont and sandhill streams in North Carolina are *K. dorsenna.* Members of this taxon are characterized by a mentum with a narrow, pointed median tooth (similar to that in *Acalcarella*) and six lateral teeth. The ventromental plates are similar to those of *Saetheria tylus,* but the premandible does not match that of *Saetheria* species.

Lauterborniella. The mobile, cased larva of *L. agrayloides* has been collected from ponds and slow-moving coastal plain rivers. *Lauterborniella* is similar to *Zavreliella.*

Lipiniella. Larval specimens have been collected from sandy substrates of reservoirs, mountain streams, and (especially) rivers. No adults have been collected in the Southeast.

Microchironomus. We collected a possible undescribed species in a North Carolina coastal river. Species in this genus were once placed in the genus *Leptochironomus.*

Micropsectra. There are no described species of *Micropsectra* in the Southeast, but at least six larval types have been found in North Carolina streams and five undescribed adults in South Carolina. *Micropsectra dubius* was listed for Alabama but was later transferred to *Paratanytarsus* (Säwedal 1982). Many investigators have used the presence of an antennal tubercle and the arrangement of claws on the posterior parapods (arranged in multiple rows for *Micropsectra*) to separate the larvae of *Micropsectra* from those of *Tanytarsus.* However, these characteristics are unreliable; characteristics of the premandible should be used instead (Pinder and Reiss 1983; Säwedal 1982). *Micropsectra* larvae are known to occur in a wide variety of lotic and lentic habitats. In the Southeast, however, they are most abundant and diverse in cool mountain streams. Some species also have been collected in the piedmont and sandhills, but *Micropsectra* is rarely collected from the coastal plain. One undescribed species is often the dominant chironomid in small mountain streams, especially in winter and early spring.

Microtendipes. Five or six species of *Microtendipes* occur in the Southeast, several of which are undescribed (N. Kirsch, personal communication). Larvae of *Micro-*
tendipes (especially those of *M. caducus* and *M. pedellus*) are widespread in clean streams, where they build long sand retreats on rocks. *Microtendipes* is a filter-feeder and one species (*pedellus*) seems to benefit from slightly enriched conditions. For example, it may be very abundant in streams influenced by agricultural runoff or dam releases. A larva similar to those of *M. rydalensis* (Pinder 1976) has a disjunct distribution in North Carolina streams, being found in both the mountain and sandhills regions. Species of *Microtendipes* are easily confused with *Apedilum elachistus,* as both taxa have a mentum with two clear median teeth; however, they can be distinguished by the shape of the pecten epipharyngis.

Unknown genus near *Microtendipes* A. This unusual larva was collected by Roback (1953) from mud and sand substrates in the Savannah River.

Unknown genus near *Microtendipes* B. This unusual larva has been characterized as a diminutive version of *Microtendipes*; it is known only from Florida. It may be a neotropical species belonging to the recently described genus *Beardius* (Reiss and Sublette 1985) or (more probably) a closely allied genus. The antenna has only five segments, the mentum has only one clear median tooth, there are only two lateral mandibular teeth, and the premandible has only two lobes.

Nilothauma. Three described species are known in the Southeast, but there are no separation characters for the larvae. Wingo (1983) suggested that a fourth species (undescribed) may occur in Lake Norman, North Carolina. An undescribed species has also been collected in several piedmont reservoirs in South Carolina.

Nimbocera. *Nimbocera pinderi* occurs throughout most of the coastal plain region, being found in lakes, rivers, and slow-moving streams. It is rarely abundant north of Florida.

Unknown genus near *Nimbocera.* The larva of a genus near *Nimbocera* was described as "*Calopsectra* sp. 13" by Roback (1966) and as "*Tanytarsus* n. subgenus A" by Steiner et al. (1982). It has been collected throughout the coastal plain in ditches, swamps, and small lakes of Florida, Georgia, and South Carolina. Morphological differences are in annulations. The petiole is annulated in *Nimbocera,* and antennal segment 2 in genus near *Nimbocera.*

Omisus. *Omisus pica* is usually in humic-water habitats in the coastal plain. The larva was described by Beck and Beck (1970). Larvae of an undescribed species have been collected from Florida and an undescribed adult from northwest Georgia.

Pagastiella. *Pagastiella ostansa* is a littoral species in ponds and lakes, where it is sometimes the dominant chironomid. It also has been collected from slow-moving areas of streams. A very pale mentum is characteristic of this genus. An undescribed species has been collected in coastal streams.

Parachironomus. Larvae of *Parachironomus* are usually found in lakes and slow-moving sections of streams. One species is often abundant in polluted North Carolina streams and rivers, although it is never dominant. Simpson and Bode (1980) illustrated this same species as *P. abortivus* and indicated that it is tolerant of combined toxic and organic wastes. Both New York and North Carolina specimens are characterized by having the seventh lateral tooth of the mentum "pale and inconspicuous." Larvae of seven southeastern species were illustrated by Beck and Beck (1969b), but species identifications are often difficult. Larvae of *P. pectinatellae* and *P. frequens* are similar but can be separated by using characteristics of the premandible (Simpson and Bode 1980). Larvae of *P. pectinatellae* have been found in bryozoans.

Paracladopelma. Larvae of *Paracladopelma* are found in coarse sand substrates of both lentic and (especially) lotic habitats. The genus was reviewed by Jackson (1977), and Saether (1979) verified that the larva of "*Cryptochironomus* near *rollei*" was equivalent to *P. doris.* A male near *P. schlitzensis* was collected at the Savannah River Plant and may be the adult of the larva figured by Jackson (1977) as *P.* sp. 1 or 2.

Paralauterborniella. The larva of *P. nigrohalteralis*, which was illustrated by Beck and Beck (1970), is widespread in streams and rivers, though never abundant (Pinder and Reiss 1983). The undescribed species is an adult collected on Lake Norman, North Carolina. *Apedilum elachistus* and *A. subcinctum* were recently transferred from *Paralauterborniella* and placed by Epler (1988a) into the genus *Apedilum*, in which they were originally described by Townes (1945).

Parapsectra. The North Carolina record is based on an adult male from the Coweeta Hydrologic Laboratory, North Carolina.

Paratanytarsus. Larvae of *Paratanytarsus* have been collected in both lotic and lentic habitats. In North Carolina, there are at least four larval types, and several of these unassociated species are widespread. Two undescribed adults have been collected from South Carolina—one from the coast and one from the mountains. Langton et al. (1988) discussed the systematics of the genus and provided a detailed account of the biology of a parthenogenetic species that should occur in the Southeast.

Paratendipes. In the Southeast, species rarely occur in lakes—contrary to information published by Pinder and Reiss (1983). Ward and Cummins (1978) provided a thorough description of the taxonomy and ecology of *P. albimanus.* Species identifications are not usually possible for larvae, but one unusual species (the *P.* "*connectens*" group of Chernovskii 1949) has been collected from rivers in North Carolina and Georgia.

Phaenopsectra. The distribution of *Phaenopsectra* in the Southeast is poorly known, partly due to taxonomic difficulties. A number of larval types are common in streams, especially from microhabitats with reduced current velocity. Work by Grodhaus (1976) indicated that some species in this genus are drought-resistant and may be semiterrestrial. The key given by Grodhaus (1987) should be used to separate *Phaenopsectra* larvae from those of *Tribelos. Phaenopsectra flavipes* is the most easily distinguished species in the larval stage. Another species, which has four equal median teeth on the mentum, occurs in mountain and piedmont areas. This larva appears to be equivalent to the *Tanytarsus* sp. 2 of Roback (1957) and the "*Phaenopsectra* prob. *dyari*" of Simpson and Bode (1980). It is not clear if this second species should be in *Tribelos* or *Phaenopsectra.* Undescribed adults have been collected in the mountains and coastal plains of South Carolina.

Polypedilum. *Polypedilum* is one of the most commonly seen genera in all aquatic habitats. Three subgenera and more than 40 species (32 described) occur in the Southeast. Species segregate according to preference for lotic or lentic habitats, ecoregion, overall habitat size (i.e., ponds versus lakes), and microhabitat. However, any given stream or river may support five or more species. There is some evidence that seasonal differences also reduce competition between coexisting species (Lenat and Folley 1983).

Three described southeastern species of the subgenus *Pentapedilum*, and several more undescribed species, occur in the coastal plain of South Carolina. This group seems to prefer small lentic waters, such as ditches and pools.

The Aufwuchs communities of most streams and rivers in the Southeast contain several species in the subgenus *Polypedilum*—especially *P. illinoense*, *P. convictum*, and *P. aviceps*. These three species are listed in the approximate order of their tolerance to organic pollution (most to least), and may also separate according to water current or ecoregion. *Polypedilum aviceps* is more common in the mountain region than in the piedmont or coastal plain, and a reduction in current has been shown to favor *P. illinoense* over *P. convictum* (Beckett and Miller 1982). Both *P. convictum* and *P. illinoense* are tolerant of sewage or toxic wastes, but *P. illinoense* replaces *P. convictum* as the stress increases (Simpson and Bode 1980).

Most species in the subgenus *Polypedilum* are either collector-filterers or collector-gatherers. However, some species have more specialized feeding habits. *Polypedilum fallax* has been associated with wood substrates (Roback 1953), *P. braseniae* is a miner in two species of macrophytes (Leathers 1922), and *P. ontario* has been collected in the cases of the caddisfly *Cheumatopsyche* (Beck 1977).

Sand substrates are frequently dominated by species in the subgenus *Tripodura*—especially *P. halterale* and *P. scalaenum*. Data from both North Carolina and New York indicate that these species (or species groups, and especially *P. scalaenum*) tolerate various pollutants. Two of the *Tripodura* species (*P. floridense* and *P. pterospilus*) seem to be limited to the extreme southern United States.

Considerable taxonomic work has been done on this group. Maschwitz (1975) gave keys for the known larvae in all subgenera and described a number of new species in the subgenus *Polypedilum*. Five of these new species have been recorded in the Southeast, but since the descriptions have not been formally published, the forms are still considered "undescribed." Boesel (1985), who reviewed the ecology and taxonomy of the northeastern species, synonymized five species that had been listed for the Southeast: *P. albulum* = *P. tritum*; *P. digitifer*, *P. griseopunctatum*, and *P. simulans* = *P. halterale*; and *P. obtusum* = *P. convictum*. Because Boesel's material was limited and his analysis regional, we do not follow his synonymies here. Soponis and Russell (1982) published helpful illustrations for all instars of three species of *Polypedilum*: *aviceps*, *convictum*, and *illinoense*.

Pontomyia. The larvae, which are marine inhabitants, are superficially similar to those of *Pseudochironomus*. A

Florida species is characterized by bifid claws on the anterior and posterior prolegs, nine teeth on the mentum, and a premandible with five lobes.

Pseudochironomus. Saether (1977b), who reviewed the taxonomy of *Pseudochironomus*, included larval descriptions for three of the five described southeastern species. He listed the preferred habitat as algae over sand and gravel. Most taxonomic work has been done with specimens from lakes, and the status of stream species is uncertain. The most commonly collected lotic species key to *P. prasinatus* gr. (consisting of two Palearctic species) in Saether (1977b). Another larva, near *P. pseudoviridis*, has been collected from a piedmont stream.

Rheotanytarsus. Larvae of *Rheotanytarsus* are often abundant in streams and rivers throughout the Southeast. They are filter-feeders favored by the addition of coarse particulate material (Kullberg 1988) and therefore may increase in abundance below some organic waste sources or below lake outlets. Two "groups," both of which are common in the Southeast, were illustrated by Simpson and Bode (1980). They indicated that the *R. exiguus* group tolerates moderate pollution. At least five undescribed adults have been collected in South Carolina and a similar number of larval types in North Carolina. This genus appears to have the greatest diversity of species in the mountain area.

Robackia. Two species are common in coarse sand substrates of southeastern streams and rivers. Although *Robackia* is found in some northern lakes, it seems to be confined to lotic habitats in the Southeast. Smith (1983) indicated that both described species have an equal number of teeth on the mentum, but there is greater overlap of the seventh lateral in *R. claviger* than in *R. demeijerei*.

Saetheria. A common inhabitant of sand substrates of oligotrophic lakes and streams is *S. tylus*, the larva of which was described by Jackson (1977). In the Southeast, however, it is found primarily in streams. *Saetheria hirta* (Saether 1983b) has been collected from one locality each in North Carolina and South Carolina. Larvae of a possible third species have been collected from a piedmont stream in North Carolina. The median tooth of the mentum was wider in these specimens than in *S. tylus*, in which it narrowed to a sharp median point.

Stelechomyia. The only southeastern species is *S. perpulchra* (= *Lauterborniella perpulchra* = Chironomini sp. A sensu Roback). Larvae are infrequently collected from wood substrates in coastal plain streams.

Stempellina. The heavy sand cases of these mobile grazers may make collection by traditional methods difficult. Larvae of some species in this genus are characterized by bizarre tubercles and projections on the head and antennae. Collections of adults indicate that at least eight species occur in the Southeast and that it is not uncommon for two or more species to coexist in the same habitat. *Stempellina* species seem to be evenly divided between lotic and lentic habitats.

Stempellinella. Tabulation of species is complicated because Pinder and Reiss (1983) used different characters to separate closely related genera than had previously been used by chironomid taxonomists in the Southeast (Steiner et al. 1982). The portable sand cases of the larvae are probably not commonly collected by traditional means. Limited collections indicated that the genus occurs in the sandhills, coastal plain, and mountains; a few records came from the piedmont.

Stenochironomus. The ecology and taxonomy of *Stenochironomus* were reviewed in detail by Borkent (1984). Most species are widespread, and it is common for several species to occur in the same stream. Many *Stenochironomus* species are collected from both lotic and lentic habitats, but usually strongly prefer one over the other. Larvae mine dead wood or dead leaves in areas of permanent water. The larvae are easily recognized; only *Xestochironomus* is similar (but it has longer anal tubules).

Stictochironomus. There are three described species of *Stictochironomus* in the Southeast; the larvae of two of these were described by Mason (1985c). The larva of *S. palliatus* is unknown. Specimens often have badly worn mouth parts, reflecting the rigors of living in sand. Wiley (1981) found that *S. virgatus* foraged for diatoms deep in the sediment, using hemoglobin to compensate for a lack of direct access to dissolved oxygen.

Sublettea. Roback (1975) described *S. coffmani*, which occurs in lotic habitats throughout the piedmont and mountains. It is rarely abundant, however, and is often confused with *Rheotanytarsus*.

Tanytarsus. *Tanytarsus* larvae are collected from most aquatic habitats in the Southeast and are often abundant. Several investigators, using information from either adults or larvae, have listed a large number of undescribed species, and it is clear that most lakes, rivers, and larger streams support 10–19 species of *Tanytarsus*. This diversity is most evident in the piedmont and coastal plains; in mountain streams *Tanytarsus* appears to be replaced by *Micropsectra*.

Unpublished keys for *Tanytarsus* larvae have been constructed for both Florida by R. P. Rutter (personal communication) and North Carolina by one of us (D. R. L.). These keys indicate at least 20 undescribed species in the Southeast and it seems likely that twice this number will eventually be recorded.

Tribelos. This genus was revised by Grodhaus (1987), who illustrated the larvae of three species. Larvae of this genus (mostly *T. jucundum*) are often abundant in coastal plain streams and are common "edge" species in most other streams and rivers. Species are rarely important in lakes in the Southeast. Larvae of *T. fuscicorne* key to *Phaenopsectra* in most keys. This species is characterized by small, narrow ventromental plates. The undescribed species are from the mountains and coastal plain of South Carolina.

Xenochironomus. Only one described species in the Southeast remains in this genus. Other species described by Roback (1963) as *Xenochironomus* have been transferred to *Axarus* or *Lipiniella*. Larvae of a possible undescribed species have been collected from the piedmont in North Carolina. *Xenochironomus xenolabis* mines in freshwater sponges and is relatively common in North Carolina. Its infrequency in collections from other areas may reflect its habitat specificity rather than its rarity.

Xestochironomus. This largely tropical genus was reviewed by Borkent (1984). The habitat of *X. subletti* is similar to that of *Stenochironomus*—mining in pieces of wood firmly attached to the bottom of coastal plain streams. Larvae of this genus are easily separated from *Stenochironomus* by the elongate anal tubules with four or five constrictions. *Xestochironomus dominicanus* identified from Lake Norman in North Carolina (Wingo 1983) were *X. subletti*.

Zavrelia. Steiner et al. (1982) suggested that, on the basis of antennal characteristics, *Zavrelia* was not present in the United States. However, Pinder and Reiss (1983), who used characters of the premandible to separate *Zavrelia* from *Stempellinella*, indicated that *Zavrelia* seems to occur in the Southeast. It seems to be restricted to cool streams of the mountains and sandhills and not confined to lentic systems (as was suggested by Pinder and Reiss 1983).

Zavreliella. This genus is similar to *Lauterborniella*. One species (*Z. varipennis*) is widespread throughout the Southeast. Larvae are abundant in some Florida freshwater marshes (D. Evans, personal communication) and eutrophic lakes and ponds.

Chironomini Genus A (Roback 1966). Larvae have been reported in marginal sediments of slow-moving rivers in Texas, Florida, Central America, and South America. This taxon also occurs in Lake Murray, South Carolina (T. J. Wilda, personal communication).

Chironomini Genus B (Pinder and Reiss 1983). Larvae of this genus have previously been reported in river sediments from New York and Kentucky. In the Southeast, they are common in the littoral sediments of Lake Norman, North Carolina (T. J. Wilda, personal communication). An associated pupa from the Mobile River, Alabama, indicates an affinity to Chironomini Genus F of Pinder and Reiss (1986).

Chironomini Genus C. Larvae of this genus have been found only in Florida and are not illustrated or described. Its characters indicate a possible placement in the *Harnischia* group, except that it has long seta-like filaments anteriorly on the mentum or in the mental area.

Summary and Conclusions

The chironomid fauna of the six southeastern States consists of 164 described genera and 479 described species. In addition we have listed 14 genera and 245 species that are tentatively noted as undescribed or are illustrated but not officially described; most of these are probably new. The percentage of undescribed species in each major subfamily is similar—27 to 37%. There are also several more undescribed genera in the Southeast. Mozley (1980) described nine larvae of questionable generic placement, of which only three have yet been associated with described genera. One of us (P.L.H.) has adult and pupal material representing seven possible new genera.

Of the 202 genera listed for the Nearctic by Ashe et al. (1987), 42 have yet to be collected in the Southeast (Table 5). Many of the genera seem to have restricted distributions or unusual habitats. For example, of the

Table 5. *Chironomid genera known from the Nearctic region but not yet collected in the Southeast.*

Tanypodinae
Arctopelopia
Deropelopia
Macropelopia
Radotanypus
Telopelopia
Xenopelopia

Podonominae
Lasiodiamesa
Parochlus
Trichotanypus

Diamesinae
Arctodiamesa
Boreoheptagyia
Protanypus
Pseudodiamesa
Pseudokiefferiella
Syndiamesa

Prodiamesinae
Monodiamesa

Orthocladiinae
Abiskomyia
Acamptocladius
Baeoctenus
Eretmoptera
Halocladius
Heterotanytarsus
Lapposmittia
Oreadomyia
Paracladius
Paralimnophyes
Parasmittia
Paratrissocladius
Parorthocladius
Tethymyia
Thalassosmittia
Trichochilus

Chironominae
Acalcarella
Beardius
Caladomyia
Corynocera
Cyphomella
Graceus
Krenopsectra
Neozavrelia
Sergentia
Skutzia

16 genera of Orthocladiinae listed in Table 5, 4 are marine inhabitants, 4 have a northern distribution, 2 have unusual habitats, and 6 have no clear-cut habitats or distribution. Continued sampling might be expected to eventually yield the following genera in the Southeast: *Acamptocladius*, *Baeoctenus*, *Beardius*, *Cyphomella*, *Lasiodiamesa*, and *Telopelopia*. More extensive sampling of marine habitats may also yield several new generic records.

Regional distributions of subfamilies indicate a higher concentration of species of Chironominae and Tanypodinae in the coastal region than in the other areas and an even distribution of Orthocladiinae from the coast to the mountains. Considering the major habitats (lakes, rivers, and streams), Tanypodinae are evenly distributed, whereas Orthocladiinae are more predominant in streams and Chironominae in lakes.

To help in describing the unknown chironomid fauna in the Southeast, benthic workers sorting samples should watch for mature pupal specimens—especially those with attached larval exuviae. These represent a complete rearing and may be the only means of getting such material from lotic situations. They should be sent to the appropriate taxonomist for identification.

> *"Human knowledge will be erased from the archives of the world before we possess the last word that a gnat has to say to us."*
>
> Attributed to Jean Henri Fabre (1823–1915) by Edwin Way Teale in *Near Horizons* (1942)

Acknowledgments

For reviewing the manuscript, providing distributional data, or offering anecdotal material on chironomid ecology, we thank B. Bilyj, Department of Fisheries and Oceans Canada, Winnipeg, Manitoba; P. S. Cranston, Commonwealth Scientific and Industrial Research Organization, Canberra, Australia; J. S. Doughman, U.S. Geological Survey, Yuma, Arizona; J. H. Epler, Florida A&M University, Tallahassee; D. L. Evans, Water and Air Research, Inc., Gainesville, Florida; L. C. Ferrington, Jr., University of Kansas, Lawrence; J. E. Gannon and S. B. Smith, National Fisheries Research Center—Great Lakes, Ann Arbor, Michigan; M. W. Heyn and C. N. Watson, Clemson University, Clemson, South Carolina; A. D. Huryn, University of Alabama, Tuscaloosa; N. Kirsch, Minnesota Department of Natural Resources, St. Paul; D. R. Oliver, Biosystematic Research Institute, Ottawa, Ontario; W. L. Pennington, University of Tennessee, Knoxville; R. P. Rutter, Kevin Erwin and Associates, Fort Myers, Florida; B. H. Tracy, Carolina Power and Light, New Hill, North Carolina; and T. J. Wilda, Duke Power Company, Huntersville, North Carolina. We also thank Marilyn Murphy, National Fisheries Research Center—Great Lakes, for capably performing word processing on numerous drafts.

References

Ashe, P. 1983. A catalogue of chironomid genera and subgenera of the world including synonyms (Diptera:Chironomidae). Entomol. Scand. Suppl. 17:1–68.

Ashe, P., D. A. Murray, and F. Reiss. 1987. The zoogeographical distribution of Chironomidae (Insecta:Diptera). Ann. Limnol. 23:27–60.

Barton, D. R., C. W. Pugsley, and H. B. N. Hynes. 1987. The life history and occurrence of *Parachaetocladius abnobaeus* (Diptera:Chironomidae). Aquat. Insects 9:189–194.

Beck, E. C., and W. M. Beck, Jr. 1969a. The Chironomidae of Florida II. The nuisance species. Fla. Entomol. 52:1–11.

Beck, E. C., and W. M. Beck, Jr. 1969b. Chironomidae (Diptera) of Florida III. The *Harnischia* complex (Chironomidae). Bull. Fla. State Mus. Biol. Sci. 13:277–313.

Beck, W. M., Jr. 1976. Biology of the larval chironomids. Fla. State Dep. Environ. Reg. Tech. Ser. 2:1–58.

Beck, W. M., Jr. 1977. Environmental requirements and pollution tolerance of common freshwater Chironomidae. U.S. Environmental Protection Agency, EPA 600/4-77-024. 261 pp.

Beck, W. M., Jr. 1980. Interesting new chironomid records for the southern United States (Diptera:Chironomidae). J. Ga. Entomol. Soc. 15:69–73.

Beck, W. M., and E. C. Beck. 1966. Chironomidae (Diptera) of Florida I. Pentaneurini (Tanypodinae). Bull. Fla. State Mus. Biol. Sci. 10:305–379.

Beck, W. M., Jr., and E. C. Beck. 1970. The immature stages of some Chironomini (Chironomidae). Q. J. Fla. Acad. Sci. 33:29–42.

Beckett, D. C., and M. C. Miller. 1982. Macroinvertebrate colonization of multiplate samplers in the Ohio River: the effect of dams. Can. J. Fish. Aquat. Sci. 39:1622–1627.

Benke, A. C., D. M. Gillespie, and F. K. Parrish. 1979. Biological basis for assessing impacts of channel modification: invertebrate production, drift, and fish feeding in a southeastern black water river. Environmental Resource Center, Georgia Institute of Technology, ERC 06-79, Atlanta, Ga.

Bilyj, B. 1985. New placement of *Tanypus pallens* Coquillett, 1902 nec *Larsia pallens* (Coq.) sensu Roback 1971 (Diptera: Chironomidae) and redescription of the holotype. Can. Entomol. 117:39–42.

Bilyj, B. 1988. A taxonomic review of *Guttipelopia* (Diptera: Chironomidae). Entomol. Scand. 19:1–26.

Bilyj, B., and I. J. Davies. 1989. Descriptions and ecological notes on seven new species of *Cladotanytarsus* (Chironomidae: Diptera) collected from an experimental acidified lake. Can. J. Zool. 67:948–962.

Bode, R. W. 1983. Larvae of North American *Eukiefferiella* and *Tvetenia* (Diptera:Chironomidae). N.Y. State Mus. Bull. 452. 40 pp.

Boesel, M. W. 1983. A review of the genus *Cricotopus* in Ohio, with a key to adults of species of the northeastern United States (Diptera:Chironomidae). Ohio J. Sci. 83:74–90.

Boesel, M. W. 1985. A brief review of the genus *Polypedilum* in Ohio, with keys to the known stages of species occurring in northeastern United States (Diptera:Chironomidae). Ohio J. Sci. 85:245–262.

Boesel, M. W., and R. W. Winner. 1980. Corynoneurinae of northeastern United States, with a key to adults and observations on their occurrence in Ohio (Diptera:Chironomidae). J. Kans. Entomol. Soc. 53:501–508.

Borkent, A. 1984. The systematics and phylogeny of the *Stenochironomus* complex (*Xestochironomus, Harrisius,* and *Stenochironomus*) (Diptera:Chironomidae). Mem. Entomol. Soc. Can. 128:1–269.

Bretschko, G. 1981. *Pontomyia* Edwards (Diptera:Chironomidae), a member of the coral reef community at Carry Bow Cay, Belize. Smithson. Contrib. Mar. Sci. 12:381–385.

Brigham, A. R., W. R. Brigham, and A. Gnilka. 1982. Aquatic insects and oligochaetes of North and South Carolina. Midwest Aquatic Enterprises, Mahomet, Ill. 837 pp.

Brundin, L. 1956. Zur Systematik der Orthocladiinae (Dipt., Chironomidae). Inst. Freshwater Res. Drottningholm Rep. 37:5–185.

Caldwell, B. A. 1984. Two new species and records of other chironomids from Georgia (Diptera:Chironomidae) with some observations on ecology. Ga. J. Sci. 42:81–96.

Caldwell, B. A. 1985. *Paracricotopus millrockensis,* a new species of Orthocladiinae (Diptera:Chironomidae) from the southeastern United States. Brimleyana 11:161–168.

Caldwell, B. A. 1986. Description of the immature stages and adult female of *Unniella multivirga* Saether (Diptera:Chironomidae) with comments on phylogeny. Aquat. Insects 8:217–222.

Carpenter, F. F. 1928. *Chironomus quadripunctatus* Malloch (Diptera:Chironomidae). Entomol. News 34:186–189.

Chernovskii, A. A. 1949. Identification of larvae of the midge family Tendipedidae. (Translation of Russian book by National Lending Library for Science and Technology, Yorkshire, England.) 299 pp.

Coffman, W. P., P. S. Cranston, D. R. Oliver, and O. A. Saether. 1986. The pupae of Orthocladiinae (Diptera: Chironomidae) of the Holarctic region. Keys and diagnoses.

Entomol. Scand. Suppl. 28:147–296.

Coffman, W. P., and L. C. Ferrington, Jr. 1984. Chironomidae. Pages 551–652 *in* R. W. Merritt and K. W. Cummins, eds. An introduction to the aquatic insects of North America. 2nd ed. Kendall/Hunt Publishing Company, Dubuque, Ia.

Coffman, W. P., L. C. Ferrington, Jr., and R. M. Seward. 1988. *Paraboreochlus stahli* sp. n., a new species of Podonominae (Diptera:Chironomidae) from the Nearctic. Aquat. Insects 10:189–200.

Coffman, W. P., and S. S. Roback. 1984. *Lopescladius* (*Cordiella*) *hyporheicus,* a new subgenus and species (Diptera: Chironomidae:Orthocladiinae). Proc. Acad. Nat. Sci. Phila. 136:130–144.

Cranston, P. S. 1982a. A key to the larvae of the British Orthocladiinae (Chironomidae). Freshwater Biol. Assoc. Sci. Publ. 45. 152 pp.

Cranston, P. S. 1982b. The metamorphosis of *Symposiocladius lignicola* (Kieffer) n. gen., n. comb., a wood mining Chironomidae (Diptera). Entomol. Scand. 13:419–429.

Cranston, P. S., and D. D. Judd. 1987. *Metriocnemus* (Diptera:Chironomidae)—An ecological survey and description of a new species. J. N. Y. Entomol. Soc. 95:534–546.

Cranston, P. S., and D. R. Oliver. 1988a. Additions and corrections to the Nearctic Orthocladiinae (Diptera:Chironomidae). Can. Entomol. 120:425–462.

Cranston, P. S., and D. R. Oliver. 1988b. Aquatic xylophagous Orthocladiinae—systematics and ecology. Spixiana Suppl. (Muench.) 14:143–154.

Cranston, P. S., D. R. Oliver, and O. A. Saether. 1983. The larvae of Orthocladiinae (Diptera:Chironomidae) of the Holarctic region. Keys and diagnoses. Entomol. Scand. Suppl. 19:149–291.

Cranston, P. S., and O. A. Saether. 1986. *Rheosmittia* (Diptera:Chironomidae) a generic validation and revision of the western Palaearctic species. J. Nat. Hist. 20:31–51.

Curry, L. L. 1958. Larvae and pupae of the species of *Cryptochironomus* (Diptera) in Michigan. Limnol. Oceanogr. 3:427–442.

Darby, R. E. 1962. Midges associated with California rice fields, with special reference to their ecology (Diptera: Chironomidae). Hilgardia 32:1–206.

Dendy, J. S., and J. E. Sublette. 1959. The Chironomidae (= Tendipedidae:Diptera) of Alabama with descriptions of six new species. Ann. Entomol. Soc. Am. 52:506–519.

Doughman, J. S. 1983. A guide to the larvae of the Nearctic Diamesinae (Diptera:Chironomidae). The genera *Boreoheptagyia, Protanypus, Diamesa,* and *Pseudokiefferiella.* U.S. Geological Survey, Water Resources Investigations Report 83-4006. 58 pp.

Doughman, J. S. 1985a. Annotated key to the genera of the tribe Diamesini (Diptera:Chironomidae). Description of the female and immatures of *Potthastia iberica* Tosio, and keys to the known species of *Potthastia.* Univ. Alsk. IWR (Inst. Water Resour.) Ser. IWR-107. 49 pp.

Doughman, J. S. 1985b. *Sympotthastia* Pagast (Diptera:Chironomidae), an update based on larvae from North Carolina, *S. diastena* (Sublette) comb. n. and other Nearctic species. Brimleyana 11:39–53.

Epler, J. H. 1987. Revision of the Nearctic *Dicrotendipes* Kieffer, 1913 (Diptera:Chironomidae). Evol. Monogr. 9:1–102.

Epler, J. H. 1988a. A reconsideration of the genus *Apedilum* Townes, 1945 (Diptera:Chironomidae). Spixiana Suppl. (Muench.) 14:105–116.

Epler, J. H. 1988b. Biosystematics of the genus *Dicrotendipes* Kieffer, 1913 (Diptera:Chironomidae:Chironominae) of the world. Mem. Am. Entomol. Soc. 36.

Fagnani, J. P., and A. R. Soponis. 1988. The occurrence of setal tufts on larvae of *Orthocladius* (*Orthocladius*) *annectens* Saether. Spixiana Suppl. (Muench.) 14:139–142.

Ferrington, L. C., Jr. 1984. Evidence for the hyporheic zone as a microhabitat of *Krenosmittia* spp. larvae (Diptera:Chironomidae). J. Freshwater Ecol. 2:353–358.

Ferrington, L. C., Jr. 1987. Microhabitat preference of larvae of three Orthocladiinae species (Diptera:Chironomidae) in Big Springs, a sand-bottom spring in the high plains of western Kansas. Entomol. Scand. Suppl. 29:361–368.

Ferrington, L. C., Jr., and O. A. Saether. 1987. Male, female, and pupa of *Oliveridia hugginsi*: n. sp. (Chironomidae: Diptera) from Kansas. J. Kans. Entomol. Soc. 60:451–461.

Fittkau, E. J., and S. S. Roback. 1983. The larvae of Tanypodinae (Diptera:Chironomidae) of the Holarctic region: Keys and diagnoses. Entomol. Scand. Suppl. 19:33–110.

Fittkau, E. J., and D. A. Murray. 1986. The pupae of Tanypodinae (Diptera:Chironomidae) of the Holarctic region: Keys and diagnoses. Entomol. Scand. Suppl. 28:31–113.

Fittkau, E. J., and D. A. Murray. 1988. *Bethbilbeckia floridensis*: a new genus and species of Macropelopiini from the eastern Nearctic. Spixiana Suppl. (Muench.) 14:253–259.

Grodhaus, G. 1976. Two species of *Phaenopsectra* with drought-resistant larvae (Diptera:Chironomidae). J. Kans. Entomol. Soc. 49:405–418.

Grodhaus, G. 1987. *Endochironomus* Kieffer, *Tribelos* Townes, *Synendotendipes*, n. gen., and *Endotribelos*, n. gen. (Diptera:Chironomidae) of the Nearctic region. J. Kans. Entomol. Soc. 60:167–247.

Halvorsen, G. A. 1982. *Saetheriella amplicristata* gen. n., sp. n., a new Orthocladiinae (Diptera:Chironomidae) from Tennessee. Aquat. Insects 4:131–136.

Halvorsen, G. A., and O. A. Saether. 1987. Redefinition and revision of the genus *Tokunagaia* Saether, 1973 (Diptera:Chironomidae). Entomol. Scand. Suppl. 29:173–188.

Halvorsen, G. A., E. Willassen, and O. A. Saether. 1982. Chironomidae (Dipt. from Ekse, western Norway). Fauna Norv. Ser. B 29:115–121.

Hamilton, A. L., O. A. Saether, and D. R. Oliver. 1969. A classification of the Nearctic Chironomidae. Fish. Res. Board Can. Tech. Rep. 124. 42 pp.

Hirvenoja, M. 1973. Revision der Gattung *Cricotopus* van der Wulp und ihrer Verwandten (Diptera, Chironomidae). Ann. Zool. Fenn. 10:1–363.

Hudson, P. L. 1987. Unusual larval habitats and life history of chironomid (Diptera) genera. Entomol. Scand. Suppl. 29:369–373.

Hudson, P. L., and S. J. Nichols. 1986. Benthic community of the Savannah River below a peaking hydropower station. J. Elisha Mitchell Sci. Soc. 102:107–121.

Jackson, G. A. 1977. Nearctic and Palaearctic *Paracladopelma* Harnisch and *Saetheria* n. gen. (Diptera:Chironomidae). J. Fish. Res. Board Can. 34:1321–1359.

Kugler, J. 1971. The developmental stages of *Leptochironomus stilifer* (Diptera:Chironomidae) and the characters of the genus *Leptochironomus*. Can. Entomol. 103:341–346.

Kullberg, A. 1988. The case, mouthparts, silk and silk formation of *Rheotanytarsus muscicola* Kieffer (Chironomidae: Tanytarsini). Aquat. Insects 10:249–255.

Langton, P. H., P. S. Cranston, and P. Armitage. 1988. The parthenogenetic midge of water supply systems, *Paratanytarsus grimmii* (Schneider) (Diptera:Chironomidae). Bull. Entomol. Res. 78:317–328.

Laurence, B. R. 1954. The larval inhabitants of cow pats. J. Anim. Ecol. 23:234–259.

Leathers, A. L. 1922. *Chironomus braseniae*, new species (Dip., Chironomidae). Entomol. News 33:8.

Lenat, D. R., and D. R. Folley. 1983. Lotic chironomids of the North Carolina mountains. Mem. Am. Entomol. Soc. 34:145–164.

LeSage, L., and A. D. Harrison. 1980. Taxonomy of *Cricotopus* species (Diptera:Chironomidae) from Salem Creek, Ontario. Proc. Entomol. Soc. Ont. 111:57–114.

Loden, M. S. 1974. Predation by chironomid (Diptera) larvae on oligochaetes. Limnol. Oceanogr. 19:156–159.

Lyakhov, S. M. 1941. A study of adaptations among rheophilous chironomids. Dokl. Akad. Nauk. SSSR 8:591–593.

Maschwitz, D. E. 1975. Revision of the Nearctic species of the subgenus *Polypedilum* (Chironomidae:Diptera). Ph.D. thesis, University of Minnesota, St. Paul. 325 pp.

Mason, P. G. 1985a. The larva of *Tvetenia vitracies* (Saether) (Diptera:Chironomidae). Proc. Entomol. Soc. Wash. 87:418–420.

Mason, P. G. 1985b. Four new species of the *Cryptochironomus fulvus* species complex (Diptera:Chironomidae). Entomol. Scand. 16:399–413.

Mason, P. G. 1985c. The larvae and pupae of *Stictochironomus marmoreus* and *S. quagga* (Diptera:Chironomidae). Can. Entomol. 117:43–48.

Mozley, S. C. 1980. Biological indicators of water quality in North Carolina. I. Guide to generic identification of orthocladiine Chironomidae (Diptera). [Unpubl. rep.] North Carolina Department of Natural Resources and Community Development, Division of Environmental Management, Raleigh. 90 pp.

Murray, D. A., and E. J. Fittkau. 1985. *Hayesomyia*, a new genus of Tanypodinae from the Holarctic (Diptera:Chironomidae). Spixiana Suppl. (Muench.) 11:195–207.

Oliver, D. R. 1981. Description of *Euryhapsis* new genus including three new species (Diptera:Chironomidae). Can.

Entomol. 113:711–722.

Oliver, D. R. 1983. The larvae of Diamesinae (Diptera: Chironomidae) of the Holarctic region. Keys and diagnoses. Entomol. Scand. Suppl. 19:115–138.

Oliver, D. R. 1985. Review of *Xylotopus* Oliver and description of *Irisobrillia* n. gen. (Diptera:Chironomidae). Can. Entomol. 117:1013–1110.

Oliver, D. R., and R. W. Bode. 1985. Descriptions of the larva and pupa of *Cardiocladius albiplumus* Saether (Diptera: Chironomidae). Can. Entomol. 117:803–809.

Oliver, D. R., and M. E. Roussel. 1982. The larvae of *Pagastia* Oliver (Diptera:Chironomidae) with description of three Nearctic species. Can. Entomol. 114:849–854.

Oliver, D. R., and M. E. Roussel. 1983. Redescription of *Brillia* Kieffer (Diptera:Chironomidae) with descriptions of Nearctic species. Can. Entomol. 115:257–279.

Pagast, F. 1933. Ueber die Metamorphosestadien von *Chironomus vulneratus* Zett. (Gruppe *Cryptochironomus* s. str.) Konowia 11:155–161.

Pinder, L. C. V. 1976. Morphology of the adult and juvenile stages of *Microtendipes rydalensis* (Edw.) comb. nov. (Diptera, Chironomidae). Hydrobiologia 48:179–184.

Pinder, L. C. V. 1978. A key to the adult males of the British Chironomidae (Diptera), the nonbiting midges. Vols. 1, 2. Freshwater Biol. Assoc. Sci. Publ. 37. 169 pp.

Pinder, L. C. V., and F. Reiss. 1983. The larvae of Chironominae (Diptera:Chironomidae) of the Holarctic region. Keys and diagnoses. Entomol. Scand. Suppl. 19:293–435.

Pinder, L. C. V., and F. Reiss. 1986. The pupae of Chironominae (Diptera:Chironomidae) of the Holarctic region. Keys and diagnoses. Entomol. Scand. Suppl. 28:299–456.

Reiss, F. 1974. Die in stehenden Gewässern der Neotropis verbreitete Chironomidengattung *Goeldichironomus* Fittkau (Diptera, Insecta). Stud. Neotrop. Fauna 9:85–122.

Reiss, F. 1982. *Hyporhygma* n. gen. und *Stelechomyia* n. gen. aus Nordamerika (Diptera,Chironomidae). Spixiana (Muench.) 5:289–302.

Reiss, F. 1988. Die Gattung *Kloosia* Kruseman, 1933 mit der Neubeschreibung zweier Arten. Spixiana Suppl. (Muench.) 14:35–44.

Reiss, F., and L. Säwedal. 1981. Keys to males and pupae of the Palaearctic (excl. Japan) *Paratanytarsus* Thienemann and Bause, 1913, n. comb., with descriptions of three new species (Diptera:Chironomidae). Entomol. Scand. Suppl. 15:73–104.

Reiss, F., and J. E. Sublette. 1985. *Beardius* new genus with notes on additional Pan-American taxa (Diptera, Chironomidae). Spixiana Suppl. (Muench.) 11:179–193.

Rempel, J. G. 1937. Notes on the genus *Chasmatonotus* with descriptions of three new species (Diptera:Chironomidae). Can. Entomol. 69:250–255.

Roback, S. S. 1953. Savannah River tendipedid larvae [Diptera: Tendipididae (Chironomidae)]. Proc. Acad. Nat. Sci. Phila. 105:91–132.

Roback, S. S. 1957. The immature tendipedids of the Philadelphia area. Monogr. Acad. Nat. Sci. Phila. 9:1–153.

Roback, S. S. 1963. The genus *Xenochironomus* (Diptera: Tendipedidae) Kieffer, taxonomy and immature stages. Trans. Am. Entomol. Soc. 88:235–245.

Roback, S. S. 1966. The Catherwood Foundation Peruvian-Amazon Expedition XII. Diptera, with some observations on the salivary glands of the Tendipedidae. Monogr. Acad. Nat. Sci. Phila. 14:305–375.

Roback, S. S. 1971. The adults of the subfamily Tanypodinae (= Pelopiinae) in North America (Diptera:Chironomidae). Monogr. Acad. Nat. Sci. Phila. 17. 410 pp.

Roback, S. S. 1974. The immature stages of the genus *Coelotanypus* (Chironomidae:Tanypodinae:Coelotanypodini) in North America. Proc. Acad. Nat. Sci. Phila. 126:9–19.

Roback, S. S. 1975. A new subgenus and species of the genus *Tanytarsus* (Chironomidae:Chironominae:Tanytarsini). Proc. Acad. Nat. Sci. Phila. 127:71–80.

Roback, S. S. 1976. The immature chironomids of the eastern United States I. Introduction and Tanypodinae—Coelotanypodini. Proc. Acad. Nat. Sci. Phila. 127:147–201.

Roback, S. S. 1977. The immature chironomids of the eastern United States II. Tanypodinae—Tanypodini. Proc. Acad. Nat. Sci. Phila. 128:55–88.

Roback, S. S. 1978. The immature chironomids of the eastern United States III. Tanypodinae—Anatopyniini, Macropelopiini, and Natarsiini. Proc. Acad. Nat. Sci. Phila. 129:151–202.

Roback, S. S. 1979. *Hudsonimyia karelena*, a new genus and species of Tanypodinae, Pentaneurini. Proc. Acad. Nat. Sci. Phila. 131:1–8.

Roback, S. S. 1980. The immature chironomids of the eastern United States IV. Tanypodinae—Procladiini. Proc. Acad. Nat. Sci. Phila. 132:1–63.

Roback, S. S. 1981. The immature chironomids of the eastern United States V. Pentaneurini — *Thienemannimyia* group. Proc. Acad. Nat. Sci. Phila. 133:73–128.

Roback, S. S. 1982a. The identity of *Ablabesmyia* sp. Roback, Bereza, and Vidrine (1980) (Diptera:Chironomidae). Entomol. News 93:13–15.

Roback, S. S. 1982b. The Tanypodinae (Diptera:Chironomidae) of Australia II. Proc. Acad. Nat. Sci. Phila. 134:80–112.

Roback, S. S. 1983. *Krenopelopia hudsoni*: a new species from the eastern United States (Diptera:Chironomidae: Tanypodinae). Proc. Acad. Nat. Sci. Phila. 135:254–256.

Roback, S. S. 1985. The immature chironomids of the eastern United States VI. Pentaneurini—genus *Ablabesmyia*. Proc. Acad. Nat. Sci. Phila. 137:153–212.

Roback, S. S. 1986a. The immature chironomids of the eastern United States VII. Pentaneurini—genus *Monopelopia*, with redescription of the male adults and description of some Neotropical material. Proc. Acad. Nat. Sci. Phila. 138:350–365.

Roback, S. S. 1986b. The immature chironomids of the eastern United States VIII. Pentaneurini and genus *Nilotanypus*, with the description of a new species from Kansas. Proc. Acad. Nat. Sci. Phila. 138:443–465.

Roback, S. S. 1986c. *Reomyia* a new genus of Tanypodinae—Pentaneurini (Diptera, Chironomidae). Spixiana (Muench.) 9:283–284.

Roback, S. S. 1987a. The immature chironomids of the eastern United States IX. Pentaneurini—genus *Labrundinia* with the description of some Neotropical material. Proc. Acad. Nat. Sci. Phila. 139:159–209.

Roback, S. S. 1987b. The immature stages and female adults of *Alotanypus aris* Roback with a redescription of the male adult (Diptera:Chironomidae:Macropelopiini). Not. Nat. (Phila.) 466. 8 pp.

Roback, S. S., and R. P. Rutter. 1988. *Denopelopia atria*, a new genus and species of Pentaneurini (Diptera:Chironomidae: Tanypodinae) from Florida. Spixiana Suppl. (Muench.) 14:117–127.

Roback, S. S., and K. J. Tennessen. 1978. The immature stages of *Djalmabatista pulcher* [= *Procladius* (*Calotanypus*) *pulcher* (Joh.)]. Proc. Acad. Nat. Sci. Phila. 130:11–20.

Rossaro, B. 1979. Description of the larva of *Paratrichocladius rufiventris* (Diptera:Chironomidae). Not. Entomol. 59:75–78.

Saether, O. A. 1969. Some Nearctic Podonominae, Diamesinae, and Orthocladiinae (Diptera:Chironomidae). Bull. Fish. Res. Board Can. 170:1–154.

Saether, O. A. 1971. Nomenclature and phylogeny of the genus *Harnischia* (Diptera:Chironomidae). Can. Entomol. 103:347–362.

Saether, O. A. 1975a. Nearctic and Palaearctic *Heterotrissocladius* (Diptera:Chironomidae). Bull. Fish. Res. Board Can. 193:1–67.

Saether, O. A. 1975b. Twelve new species of *Limnophyes* Eaton, with keys to Nearctic males of the genus (Diptera:Chironomidae). Can. Entomol. 107:1029–1056.

Saether, O. A. 1976. Revision of *Hydrobaenus*, *Trissocladius*, *Zalutschia*, *Paratrissocladius*, and some related genera (Diptera: Chironomidae). Bull. Fish. Res. Board Can. 195:1–287.

Saether, O. A. 1977a. Female genitalia in Chironomidae and other Nematocera: morphology, phylogenies, keys. Bull. Fish. Res. Board Can. 197:1–211.

Saether, O. A. 1977b. Taxonomic studies on Chironomidae: *Nanocladius*, *Pseudochironomus*, and the *Harnischia* complex. Bull. Fish. Res. Board Can. 196:1–143.

Saether, O. A. 1979. *Paracladopelma doris* (Townes) [syn. "*Cryptochironomus*" near *rollei* (Saether 1977) n. syn.] and *P. rollei* (Kirpichenko) n. comb. (Diptera:Chironomidae). Entomol. Scand. Suppl. 10:117–118.

Saether, O. A. 1980a. The females and immatures of *Paracricotopus* Thienemann and Harnisch, 1932, with the description of a new species (Diptera:Chironomidae). Aquat. Insects 2:129–145.

Saether, O. A. 1980b. Three female chironomid genitalia (Diptera). Pages 115–121 *in* D. A. Murray, ed. Chironomidae. Pergamon Press, New York.

Saether, O. A. 1981a. *Doncricotopus bicaudatus* n. gen., n. sp. (Diptera:Chironomidae, Orthocladiinae) from the North-west Territories, Canada. Entomol. Scand. 12:223–229.

Saether, O. A. 1981b. Orthocladiinae (Chironomidae:Diptera) from the British West Indies with descriptions of *Antillocladius* n. gen., *Lipurometriocnemus* n. gen., *Compterosmittia* n. gen., and *Diplosmittia* n. gen. Entomol. Scand. Suppl. 16:1–46.

Saether, O. A. 1982. Orthocladiinae (Diptera:Chironomidae) from SE U.S.A., with descriptions of *Plhudsonia*, *Unniella* and *Platysmittia* n. genera and *Atelopodella* n. subgen. Entomol. Scand. 13:465–510.

Saether, O. A. 1983a. A review of Holarctic *Gymnometriocnemus* Goetghebuer, 1932, with the description of *Raphidocladius* subgen. n. and *Sublettiella* gen. n. (Diptera:Chironomidae). Aquat. Insects 5:209–226.

Saether, O. A. 1983b. *Oschia dorsenna* n. gen., n. sp. and *Saetheria hirta* n. sp., two new members of the *Harnischia* complex (Diptera:Chironomidae). Entomol. Scand. 14:395–404.

Saether, O. A. 1984. The immatures of *Antillocladius* Saether, 1981 (Diptera:Chironomidae). Aquat. Insects 6:1–6.

Saether, O. A. 1985a. *Heleniella parva* sp. n. (Diptera:Chironomidae) from South Carolina and Tennessee. Entomol. Scand. 15:532–535.

Saether, O. A. 1985b. *Apometriocnemus fontinalis* gen. n., sp. n. (Diptera:Chironomidae) from Tennessee. Entomol. Scand. 15:536–539.

Saether, O. A. 1985c. The imagines of *Mesosmittia* Brundin, 1956, with description of seven new species. Spixiana (Muench.) 11:37–54.

Saether, O. A. 1985d. A review of the genus *Rheocricotopus* Thienemann and Harnisch, 1932, with the description of three new species. Spixiana (Muench.) 11:59–108.

Saether, O. A. 1985e. The females of *Compteromesa oconeensis* Saether, 1981, and *Prodiamesa olivacea* (Meigens 1818) (syn. *Trichodiamesa autumnalis* Goetghebuer, 1926, n. syn.). Spixiana (Muench.) 11:7–13.

Saether, O. A. 1985f. Redefinition and review of *Thienemannia* Kieffer, 1909 (Diptera:Chironomidae), with the description of *T. pilinucha* sp. n. Aquat. Insects 7:111–131.

Saether, O. A. 1985g. A review of *Odontomesa* Pagast, 1945 (Diptera, Chironomidae, Prodiamesinae). Spixiana (Muench.) 11:15–29.

Saether, O. A. 1985h. *Diplosmittia carinata* spec. nov. from Michigan. Spixiana (Muench.) 11:55–57.

Saether, O. A. 1989. *Metriocnemus* van der Wulp: a new species and a revision of species described by Meigen, Zetterstedt, Staeger, Holmgren, Lundstrum, and Strenzke (Diptera: Chironomidae). Entomol. Scand. 19:393–430.

Saether, O. A. 1990. A review of the genus *Limnophyes* Eaton from the Holarctic and Afrotropical regions (Diptera: Chironomidae, Orthocladiinae). Entomol. Scand. Suppl. 35. In press.

Saether, O. A., and G. A. Halvorsen. 1981. Diagnoses of *Tvetenia* Kieff. emend., *Dratnalia* n. gen., and *Eukiefferiella* Thien. emend., with a phylogeny of the *Cardiocladius* group (Diptera:Chironomidae). Entomol. Scand. Suppl. 15:269–285.

Saether, O. A., and J. E. Sublette. 1983. A review of the genera *Doithrix* n. gen., *Georthocladius* Strenzke, *Parachaetocladius* Wülker and *Pseudorthocladius* Goetghebuer (Diptera:Chironomidae, Orthocladiinae). Entomol. Scand. Suppl. 20:1–100.

Säwedal, L. 1982. Taxonomy, morphology, phylogenetic relationships and distribution of *Micropsectra* Kieffer, 1909 (Diptera:Chironomidae). Entomol. Scand. 13:371–400.

Simpson, K. W., and R. W. Bode. 1980. Common larvae of Chironomidae (Diptera) from New York State streams and rivers. N.Y. State Mus. Bull. 439:1–105.

Simpson, K. W., R. W. Bode, and P. Albu. 1983. Keys for the genus *Cricotopus* adapted from "Revision der Gattung *Cricotopus* van der Wulp und ihrer Verwandten (Diptera: Chironomidae)" by M. Hirvenoja. N.Y. State Mus. Bull. 450:1–133.

Smith, D. 1983. A note on *Robackia*. Southeast. Water Pollut. Biol. Assoc. Newsl. 7(2):11–12.

Soponis, A. R. 1977. A revision of the Nearctic species of *Orthocladius* (*Orthocladius*) van der Wulp (Diptera:Chironomidae). Mem. Entomol. Soc. Can. 102:1–187.

Soponis, A. R. 1979. *Zalutschia briani* n. sp. from Florida (Diptera:Chironomidae). Entomol. Scand. Suppl. 10:125–131.

Soponis, A. R., and C. L. Russell. 1982. Identification of instars and species in some larval *Polypedilum* (*Polypedilum*) (Diptera:Chironomidae). Hydrobiologia 94:25–32.

Steiner, J. W. 1983. *Paracricotopus mozleyi* n. sp. from Georgia, U.S.A. (Diptera:Chironomidae). Mem. Am. Entomol. Soc. 34:329–335.

Steiner, J. W., and J. L. Hulbert. 1982. *Nimbocera pinderi*, a new species (Diptera:Chironomidae) from the southeastern United States. Fla. Entomol. 65:228–233.

Steiner, J. W., J. S. Doughman, and C. R. Moore. 1982. A generic guide to the larvae of the Nearctic Tanytarsini. U.S. Geol. Surv. Open File Rep. 82-768. 40 pp.

Strenzke, K. 1950. Systematik, Morphologie, und Ökologie der terrestrischen Chironomiden. Arch. Hydrobiol. Suppl. 18:207–414.

Sublette, J. E. 1964. Chironomidae (Diptera) of Louisiana I. Systematics and immature stages of some lentic chironomids of west-central Louisiana. Tulane Stud. Zool. 11:109–150.

Sublette, J. E., and M. F. Sublette. 1973. The morphology of *Glyptotendipes barbipes* (Staeger) (Diptera:Chironomidae). Stud. Nat. Sci. (Portales, N.M.) 6:1–80.

Sublette, J. E., and M. F. Sublette. 1974. A review of the genus *Chironomus* (Diptera:Chironomidae) VII. The morphology of *Chironomus stigmaterus* Say. Stud. Nat. Sci. (Portales, N.M.) 10:1–64.

Tennessen, K. J., and P. K. Gottfried. 1983. Variation in structure of ligula of Tanypodinae larvae (Diptera:Chironomidae). Entomol. News 94:109–116.

Thienemann, A. 1926. Hydrobiologische Untersuchungen an den kalten Quellen and Bächen der Halbinsel Jasmund auf Rügen. Arch. Hydrobiol. 17:221–336.

Tokeshi, M. 1986. Population ecology of the commensal chironomid *Epoicocladius flavens* on its mayfly host *Ephemera danica*. Freshwater Biol. 16:235–243.

Townes, H. K., Jr. 1945. The Nearctic species of Tendipedini. Am. Midl. Nat. 34:1–206.

Tuiskunen, J. 1985. A description of *Psilometriocnemus europaeus* sp. n. and *Doncricotopus dentatus* sp. n. (Diptera, Chironomidae, Orthocladiinae) from Finland. Ann. Entomol. Fenn. 51:101–104.

Walshe, B. M. 1951. The feeding habits of certain chironomid larvae (subfamily Tendipedinae). Proc. Zool. Soc. Lond. 121:63–79.

Ward, G. M., and K. W. Cummins. 1978. Life history and growth pattern of *Paratendipes albimanus* in a Michigan headwater stream. Ann. Entomol. Soc. Am. 71:272–284.

Webb, C. J., J. Martin, and W. Wülker. 1987. Ultrastructure of larval ventromental plates of European and North American representatives of *Chironomus* Meigen (subgenus *Chaetolabis* Townes) (Diptera:Chironomidae). Entomol. Scand. 18:205–211.

Webb, C. J., and A. Scholl. 1985. Identification of larvae of European species of *Chironomus* Meigen (Diptera:Chironomidae) by morphological characters. Syst. Entomol. 10:353–372.

Webb, D. W. 1969. New species of chironomids from Costello Lake, Ontario (Diptera:Chironomidae). J. Kans. Entomol. Soc. 42:91–108.

Webb, D. W. 1982. *Smittia lasiops* (Malloch): a redescription of the adults with a description of the immature stages (Diptera:Chironomidae). Proc. Entomol. Soc. Wash. 84:468–474.

Wiederholm, T., editor. 1983. Chironomidae of the Holarctic region. Keys and diagnoses. Part 1. Larvae. Entomol. Scand. Suppl. 19:1–457.

Wiederholm, T., editor. 1986. Chironomidae of the Holarctic region. Keys and diagnoses. Part 2. Pupae. Entomol. Scand. Suppl. 28:1–482.

Wiederholm, T., editor. 1989. The adult males of Chironomidae (Diptera) of the Holarctic region. Keys and diagnoses. Entomol. Scand. Suppl. 34:1–532.

Wiley, M. J. 1981. An analysis of some factors influencing the successful penetration of sediment by chironomid larvae. Oikos 36:296–302.

Wingo, P. S. 1983. Species composition and emergence patterns of midges (Diptera:Chironomidae) in the vicinity of the McGuire Nuclear Station, Lake Norman, North Carolina, USA. M.S. thesis, University of North Carolina, Charlotte. 175 pp.

Wirth, W. W. 1949. A revision of the Clunioninae midges with descriptions of a new genus and four new species (Diptera, Tendipedidae). Univ. Calif. Publ. Entomol. 8:151–182.

Wirth, W. W. 1952. Notes on marine midges from the eastern United States (Diptera:Tendipedidae = Chironomidae). Bull. Mar. Sci. Gulf Caribb. 2:307–312.

Wirth, W. W., and J. E. Sublette. 1970. A review of the Podonominae of North America with descriptions of three new species of *Trichotanypus* (Diptera:Chironomidae). J. Kans. Entomol. Soc. 43:335–354.

Wülker, W. F., J. E. Sublette, M. F. Sublette, and J. Martin. 1971. A review of the genus *Chironomus* (Diptera:Chironomidae) I. The *staegeri* group. Stud. Nat. Sci. (Portales, N.M.) 1:1–88.

Yamamoto, M. 1987. Notes on the genus *Chaetolabis* Townes, status nov., with a redescription of *C. macani* (Freeman) (Diptera:Chironomidae). Esakia 25:149–154.

Hudson, Patrick L., David R. Lenat, Broughton A. Caldwell, and David Smith. 1990. **Chironomidae of the Southeastern United States: A Checklist of Species and Notes on Biology, Distribution, and Habitat.** U.S. Fish Wildl. Serv., *Fish. Wildl. Res.* 7. 46 pp.

This checklist of the species of midges (Diptera:Chironomidae) in the southeastern United States (Alabama, Florida, Georgia, North Carolina, South Carolina, and Tennessee) documents the species distribution, general habitat, and taxonomic references to facilitate the identification or description of species and genera. Changes in nomenclature, unique ecological traits, and bibliographic sources are summarized. Of the 10 subfamilies currently recognized in the Chironomidae, 7 occur in the Southeast. The chironomid fauna of the region now consists of 164 described genera and 479 described species. We also list 14 genera and 245 species that are not yet described.

Key words: Chironomidae, Chironominae, Orthocladiinae, Tanypodinae, habitats, midges, southeastern United States.

Hudson, Patrick L., David R. Lenat, Broughton A. Caldwell, and David Smith. 1990. **Chironomidae of the Southeastern United States: A Checklist of Species and Notes on Biology, Distribution, and Habitat.** U.S. Fish Wildl. Serv., *Fish. Wildl. Res.* 7. 46 pp.

This checklist of the species of midges (Diptera:Chironomidae) in the southeastern United States (Alabama, Florida, Georgia, North Carolina, South Carolina, and Tennessee) documents the species distribution, general habitat, and taxonomic references to facilitate the identification or description of species and genera. Changes in nomenclature, unique ecological traits, and bibliographic sources are summarized. Of the 10 subfamilies currently recognized in the Chironomidae, 7 occur in the Southeast. The chironomid fauna of the region now consists of 164 described genera and 479 described species. We also list 14 genera and 245 species that are not yet described.

Key words: Chironomidae, Chironominae, Orthocladiinae, Tanypodinae, habitats, midges, southeastern United States.

Hudson, Patrick L., David R. Lenat, Broughton A. Caldwell, and David Smith. 1990. **Chironomidae of the Southeastern United States: A Checklist of Species and Notes on Biology, Distribution, and Habitat.** U.S. Fish Wildl. Serv., *Fish. Wildl. Res.* 7. 46 pp.

This checklist of the species of midges (Diptera:Chironomidae) in the southeastern United States (Alabama, Florida, Georgia, North Carolina, South Carolina, and Tennessee) documents the species distribution, general habitat, and taxonomic references to facilitate the identification or description of species and genera. Changes in nomenclature, unique ecological traits, and bibliographic sources are summarized. Of the 10 subfamilies currently recognized in the Chironomidae, 7 occur in the Southeast. The chironomid fauna of the region now consists of 164 described genera and 479 described species. We also list 14 genera and 245 species that are not yet described.

Key words: Chironomidae, Chironominae, Orthocladiinae, Tanypodinae, habitats, midges, southeastern United States.

Hudson, Patrick L., David R. Lenat, Broughton A. Caldwell, and David Smith. 1990. **Chironomidae of the Southeastern United States: A Checklist of Species and Notes on Biology, Distribution, and Habitat.** U.S. Fish Wildl. Serv., *Fish. Wildl. Res.* 7. 46 pp.

This checklist of the species of midges (Diptera:Chironomidae) in the southeastern United States (Alabama, Florida, Georgia, North Carolina, South Carolina, and Tennessee) documents the species distribution, general habitat, and taxonomic references to facilitate the identification or description of species and genera. Changes in nomenclature, unique ecological traits, and bibliographic sources are summarized. Of the 10 subfamilies currently recognized in the Chironomidae, 7 occur in the Southeast. The chironomid fauna of the region now consists of 164 described genera and 479 described species. We also list 14 genera and 245 species that are not yet described.

Key words: Chironomidae, Chironominae, Orthocladiinae, Tanypodinae, habitats, midges, southeastern United States.

U.S. GOVERNMENT PRINTING OFFICE: 1990-773-216/20010